T0339631

Reputation Management Online

This book examines the work of the public relations, technology, and legal professionals who provide online "reputation management" services, situating their work within contemporary debates about regulating speech on the internet.

The author argues that legal solutions like the European "Right to Be Forgotten" are not really possible in the United States, but that the private solutions of reputation management help to ameliorate novel concerns about reputation. At the same time, he contends that these practices prompt different free speech and dignitary concerns unique to the digital environment. Drawing upon rhetorical and legal analysis of diverse texts, including reputation management promotional materials, interviews with practitioners, legal cases, and popular online commentary about reputational disputes themselves, the book intervenes in specific debates about the regulation of the internet, as well as broader socio-legal debates about the role of reputation-damaging speech in a democratic society.

This timely and relevant study will have great relevance for all students and scholars of communication studies, public relations, rhetoric, new and digital media, internet law, technology and society, computer-mediated communication, and sociology.

Ben Medeiros is Assistant Professor of Communication Studies at SUNY Plattsburgh, USA.

NCA Focus on Communication Studies
National Communication Association

Reputation Management Online

America's "Right to Be Forgotten"

Ben Medeiros

Routledge
Taylor & Francis Group

NEW YORK AND LONDON

First published 2022
by Routledge
605 Third Avenue, New York, NY 10158

and by Routledge
4 Park Square, Milton Park, Abingdon, Oxon, OX14 4RN

Routledge is an imprint of the Taylor & Francis Group, an informa business

Library of Congress Cataloging-in-Publication Data
A catalog record for this title has been requested

ISBN: 9781032262550 (hbk)
ISBN: 9781032262529 (pbk)
ISBN: 9781003287384 (ebk)

DOI: 10.4324/9781003287384

Typeset in Times New Roman
by codeMantra

Contents

Introduction

In 2010, photographs of Virginia congressional candidate Krystal Ball surfaced from a party at which she appeared dressed in a marginally risque costume. She lost the race, and there was speculation that the minor scandal around the photographs played a role. As she recently recounted to journalist Kashmir Hill, she assumed at the time that situations like hers would later appear a "temporary blip before society adjusted and 'people would grow more accepting' of photos and problematic comments from the past."[1] Eleven years later, Ball, now the co-host of The Hill's morning talk show "Rising," has instead concluded that "'[i]t's the polar opposite...[i]t's more reactionary and judgmental than it's ever been.'" Indeed, a debate about so-called "cancel culture"[2] rages as of this writing in 2021, and we have witnessed a proliferation of stories like that of Emily Wilder, who was fired from the Associated Press in 2021 after photographs and social media posts from her pro-Palestinian activism during college surfaced.[3] It seems safe to say, then, that cultural, technical, and legal questions surrounding the management of digital reputational information are more urgent than ever.

Whether for good or ill, the widespread perception in the present is that the internet has re-calibrated the balance between reputation protection and freedom of expression. Default structural aspects of the information ecosystem prior to the advent of search engines, user-generated content platforms, and the relatively limitless storage capacity of computers acted as an invisible guarantor of obscurity in many situations. Court records and old newspaper articles still existed, but they were largely out of view. The records of our fleeting transgressions, most intimate embarrassments, and interpersonal disagreements now routinely show up as the pieces of information that are most prominently associated with our digital identities.

The policy initiative to address the reputational fragility of the digital age that has received perhaps the most attention is the "Right to

DOI: 10.4324/9781003287384-1

Be Forgotten" in the European Union. In fact, the phrase has itself become a kind of shorthand for restoration of control over one's digital image. In the United States, it is sometimes invoked less as a literal reference to the specific set of provisions in the European law (which are numerous, and are discussed extensively in Chapter 3), and more in an informal sense to signify any opportunity to petition for the alteration or removal of personally identifying content that is visible on digital platforms.[4] In an age when these information trails have become not just visible but *foregrounded* in the construction of our digital identities, the law in the United States, on the other hand, has largely not adapted to provide corresponding remedies.

Despite the absence of an official "Right to Be Forgotten" in the United States, the legal system in the United States has itself long provided limited redress for reputational injury. The torts of defamation, which deals with false statements of fact, and public disclosure of private facts, which deals with statements that are true but highly personal, embarrassing, and not newsworthy, recognize that the state in a well-ordered society must protect its citizens from reputational harm. At the same time, legally sanctioned reputational redress must be carefully calibrated, as too much of it can threaten both the ability of speakers to express themselves and – arguably more importantly in a liberal democratic society – the ability of readers and listeners to seek information and expose themselves to diverse viewpoints. The perception in the present is simply that the traditional balance between these competing interests has been disrupted by the reputational precariousness of the internet. But what if other forces have also adapted to help correct this imbalance?

The foundational premise of this book is that the practices associated with "reputation management" have evolved to fill the gap between legal remedies and reputational vulnerability instead. "Reputation management" involves a number of often- but not always-overlapping practices. In this book, I use the term somewhat more capaciously than is sometimes customary: herein, it simply refers to any practice undertaken with the objective of changing the repository of information about an individual that is publicly visible through digital platforms. As such, this therefore encompasses a constellation of practices that transcend a single professional domain. The companies operating in this space themselves reflect such a conception of reputation management in their descriptions of their services. For a characteristic illustration, the company Reputation Rhino describes how it "has a team of experienced public relations, legal, marketing, and technology professionals" who do its work.[5]

The book pursues its argument by empirically documenting the ways in which the RTBF in the EU and the practices of reputation management in the United States are discursively framed in similar ways and are used to achieve similar effects. More specifically, they share a common focus on influencing the composition of the search engine results associated with an entity (either individual or business) – whether they pursue this "influence" through platforms' own terms of use, strategic leveraging of the platforms' algorithms, or even interpersonal persuasion. In this sense, reputation management practices act as an "American right to be forgotten" – simply one that is achieved through somewhat different means.

The seminal scholarship of Nora Draper has provided a very useful historical trajectory of the evolution in this field of professional services (though her book traces the somewhat more capacious collection of services that she calls the "consumer privacy industry"). She specifically lays out a progression from a shared focus on "protection" of privacy throughout the 1990s, where "early entrants in the field tended to focus on visibility as an unwanted result of institutional privacy abuses," to more of a focus on "promotion" of an ideal online image, where practitioners stress "designing, controlling, and leveraging a carefully crafted digital image" following the advent of social networking and a gradual rejection in American culture of the notion that our anonymous identities in "cyberspace" were "a world apart" from our public identities in physical space.[6] What Draper calls the "leading online reputation management company," Reputation Defender, was founded in 2006, and these are the sorts of companies that are the focus of this book.[7] Further, her account of the mentality underlying the shift in focus for this second generation of companies captures the distinctly neoliberal[8] flavor of the more contemporary discourse around reputation, where reputation management professionals gravely enumerate the unprecedented risks of the digital age but also encourage their audiences to "harness the power of reputation" rather than simply try to minimize damage.

As Draper's foundational research has also established, practitioners seem hesitant to recognize themselves as part of a unified "industry."[9] What unifies the providers of these services in her account is more an *ideology* than any set of rigidly standardized practices. She argues that this is instantiated in the form of "a type of cross talk around a set of ideologies about the politics of information ownership and the importance of self-presentation online."[10] The upshot of this ascendant pseudo-industrial ideology for Draper is that "this collection of companies has helped normalize online visibility as a requirement of contemporary life."[11]

Such a characterization is astute, but it ultimately formulates the impact of the industry in terms of the way it encourages – and perhaps normalizes – a particularly instrumental way of thinking about *one's own* digital identity management. It therefore leaves room to more thoroughly explore how the work that these companies do has a *regulatory* function (in the general sense of the word).[12] In the endeavor to provide reputational vindication for clients, what impact does reputation management have on the kind of information that is visible to the public, and on the range of discussion that is represented – in short, on what is often referred to in political theory as the "marketplace of ideas?" Draper's work itself implicitly prompts further inquiry into this dimension of the issue, as she introduces some relevant concerns about the effects of reputation management on the marketplace of ideas but ultimately truncates the inquiry, concluding simply that the "line between information management and censorship is a thin one, and where it should be drawn is not always clear."[13]

Through both their words and actions, practitioners of reputation management give us the tools to at least assess how that question tends to be answered. First, while there is certainly not a single standard formula for reputation management, there are recurring practices and assumptions about the boundaries of the endeavor. The empirical research for the book, which involved interviewing professionals who offer reputation management services and textually analyzing the voluminous body of digital content that these professionals use to promote their services, revealed a loose tripartite typology of the tactics used: efforts to affect the composition of search results through search engine optimization, efforts to negotiate with the publishers or hosts of materials deemed to be harmful, and tactics that either use legal procedures or simply provide documentation to justify removal based on the platforms' own content policies.

These practices combine with a related but distinct register of what Draper called the "cross talk...about the politics of information ownership" that is visible in reputation management professionals' descriptions of their work: specifically, a hegemonic American formulation of what it means to achieve reputational *justice* in the digital age. It conceives of the particular suite of promotion and publicity tools that reputation management offers as performing a *compensatory* function that helps to correct the contemporary imbalance between freedom of information and reputation protection. In turn, tracing the ways in which this conception of "justice" is promoted and materially pursued by reputation management practitioners allows us to then contextualize it in comparison with policy responses to the unique reputational challenges of the digital age such as the Right to Be Forgotten.

The book carries out its exploration across four chapters. The first introduces the general balance between reputation protection (or promotion) and freedom of expression in American law and public relations ethics, and some of the core objectives that these various doctrines aim to achieve. These provide the basis for assessing the different responses to the current state of perceived reputational precariousness, the contours of which are established in Chapter 2. The third and fourth chapters then compare and contrast the approach to remedying this precariousness that is taken via the Right to Be Forgotten and the approaches pursued in the United States under the guise of reputation management.

Notes

1 Kashmir Hill, "Our Digital Pasts Weren't Supposed to be Weaponized Like This." *New York Times*, May 30, 2021. https://www.nytimes.com/2021/05/29/technology/emily-wilder-firing-ap.html.

2 The term generally refers to the act of "calling out others on social media" for perceived social transgressions, but the debate over its meaning concerns its connotations. A Pew survey in late 2020 found, for instance, that while some (more commonly right-leaning) respondents associated the term with the idea of "censorship of speech or history" and "mean-spirited actions taken to cause harm to others," respondents also commonly associated it more with the idea of "actions taken to hold others accountable" (though left-leaning respondents mentioned this definition more frequently, it was also the most common answer from right-leaning respondents). And for some on both the right and left, it represents not really a wholly new phenomenon per se, but rather a form of aggressively enforced political correctness via social media bandwagoning. See https://www.pewresearch.org/internet/2021/05/19/americans-and-cancel-culture-where-some-see-calls-for-accountability-others-see-censorship-punishment/.

3 Hill, "Our Digital Pasts."

4 As will be discussed in detail in Chapter 4, for instance, the website Cleveland.com refers to its new mechanism allowing subjects of previous crime stories to petition for their removal as its "right to be forgotten." And in a different context, the venerable technology blog Techdirt referred to a scheme involving fraudulent copyright infringement takedown notices as an "illicit form of a 'right to be forgotten.'" This book therefore uses "right to be forgotten" (lower case) to refer to this idea in this more popularly invoked thematic sense (with "Right to Be Forgotten" therefore used to refer to the specific law in the European Union). https://www.cleveland.com/opinion/2018/07/right_to_be_forgotten_clevelan.html; https://www.techdirt.com/articles/20200517/17260644514/copyright-as-censorship-wsj-identifies-hundreds-bogus-news-takedowns-people-blame-google-rather-than-copyright.shtml.

5 https://www.reputationrhino.com/our-solutions/ripoffreport-removal/.

6 Nora Draper, *The Identity Trade*. New York: NYU Press (2019), 39, 104.

7 Draper, *The Identity Trade*, 106.

8 While the conceptual coordinates of neoliberalism will be discussed in more detail in Chapter 2, the cultural studies scholar Lisa Duggan captures the way in which neoliberal ideology encompasses both an economic as well as cultural sensibility, with "privatization and personal responsibility" representing its two central organizing principles. Lisa Duggan, *The Twilight of Equality*. Boston, MA: Beacon Press (2003), 12.

9 Draper, *The Identity Trade*, 38.

10 Draper, *The Identity Trade*, 39.

11 Draper, *The Identity Trade*, 135.

12 "Regulation" can be understood in abstract terms as simply forces that constrain behavior. According to Lawrence Lessig, for instance, "regulation" online happens along four axes. Laws certainly represent one, but other important forces of regulation include norms, the market, and what he calls code (basically technical architecture). See Lawrence Lessig, *Code and Other Laws of Cyberspace*. New York: Basic Books (1999), 85–86.

13 Draper, *The Identity Trade*, 156.

1 Balancing Speech and Reputation Protection

Conceptual Foundations

The goal of this chapter is threefold. First, it introduces reputation as a social phenomenon and explains why it has long been a component of human social organization even under quite disparate conditions. Second, it then establishes the role of the state in regulating the information that pertains to citizens' reputations and offering some sort of redress for undue reputational injury. In the process, we are thus introduced to the conflict that is central to assessing any system (whether via legal institutions or other means) of reputational dispute resolution: balancing the need for a pluralistic and inclusive "marketplace of ideas" in a liberal democratic society and the imperative to protect reputation as a means of facilitating human flourishing. Finally, the chapter considers the conceptual variables that pertain to both legal resolution and systems of "private ordering," exploring the advantages and disadvantages that scholars in law and political theory have associated with each.

What Is Reputation and Why Is It Important?

Reputation is an ancient phenomenon, and one that social and natural scientists have studied in myriad contexts. Some have even suggested that it represents a kind of hard-wired principle of human social organization: science writer John Whitfield, for instance, describes reputation as "deeply embedded in our biology."[1] Across the different contexts in which reputation has been studied, a central refrain is that reputation helps to sort the trustworthy from the untrustworthy for purposes of coordination. Humans use these judgments to make decisions about collaboration with others. According to Whitfield, for instance, the instincts to assess and cultivate reputations perhaps come so readily to us because "reputation's ability to encourage good behavior and deter bad, as well as deciding our success as individuals,

DOI: 10.4324/9781003287384-2

is a vital part of a well-functioning society." A similar principle can be expressed in the nomenclature of economics: "an individual's reputation provides 'a basis for inducing others to engage in market or non-market transactions' with the individual."[2] Such functions have only grown in importance with the rise of modern societies in which we must collaborate with strangers and routinely make decisions based on second-hand (i.e. not directly observed) information. Finally, business journalist Chris Komisarjevsky offers a pithier definition: "[a]t its simplest, [reputation] is what others think of us."[3]

Reputation thus fundamentally inheres in the judgments that *others* make based on available information. For this reason, we may seek to influence it through our actions, but it is not "ours" in the most fundamental sense. Philosopher Gloria Origgi thus asserts that

> the control we wield over our reputation is limited and precarious...because the multiplicity of real and imaginary social 'mirrors' that reflect it back and forth among themselves and then back to us distorts it, rendering it elusive, shape-shifting, and ineffable.[4]

Given this characteristic, the norms and rules that develop around the management of reputational information are thus critical to ensure that judgments are both useful as well as fair.

Much of the resolution in everyday life is informal: it is through reputation mechanisms such as gossip, peer mediation, and broadcast (i.e. one-to-many) publicity that information about individuals is often circulated, vetted for accuracy and credibility, and countered. This is sensible, as the machinery of the state is expensive to engage (thus sometimes making private resolution the only cost-justified solution) and governments traditionally relinquish some private domain into which public rules do not directly penetrate (even if, again, this might only be so because enforcement costs would be prohibitive). Yet informal systems alone may not fully deter or compensate for the malicious or reckless dissemination of reputational information, and informal resolution often leaves little public record, thus potentially making it less valuable as an informational signal to future collaborators.[5]

Balancing Reputation Defense and Freedom of Expression in US Law

A well-ordered society thus requires the state to help settle disputes pertaining to reputationally damaging speech first and foremost because commitments to public order and the rule of law require some formalized alternative to the honor killings and clan warfare that might otherwise erupt over reputational disputes. Beyond mitigating the general disturbance of public order, another function of law is to provide victims with some means of vindication when they are unfairly maligned. The civil law has therefore long sought to separate innocent or productive speech about others from injurious and actionable assertions in order to protect the reputational interests of citizens.

In the United States, as many readers will already be aware, the area of law traditionally associated with regulating speech that threatens reputational harm is the tort of defamation, the crux of which concerns false statements of fact about another person. (Slander is spoken defamation; libel is written defamation.) In practice, most litigation and consequently most debates in modern US defamation law have concerned libel. Defamation is the product of centuries of common law evolution, and for much of its history imposed a strict liability standard, meaning essentially that anyone found to have made defamatory statements was subject to liability regardless of whether it was done purposefully, recklessly, or accidentally.

The common law typically required four criteria to be met in a successful defamation action: (1) a false statement of fact (i.e. one that is neither true nor an opinion which cannot be proven true or false) that (2) refers to or "concerns" the plaintiff, and (3) was published to a third party with (4) the effect of causing harm to the subject of the statement. Along with added considerations of fault (discussed below), each of these elements generally must still be demonstrated to win a defamation judgment today.

In justifying the state's interest in allowing compensation for defamation as a civil injury, commentators and judges have often invoked some combination of material and dignitary interests. The material interests involve the actual consequences of a so-called "damaged reputation": the victim might lose their job or have a hard time finding another one, be shunned by their friends, and be subsequently dogged by suspicion in whatever future dealings. This is not, however, the only kind of harm that defamation law has contemplated over time. In fact, a significant amount of the state's interest in protecting reputation seems to be aimed at ameliorating the psychological effects of being falsely associated with some kind of perfidious behavior or condition.[6] In practice, therefore, defamation law essentially addresses a combination of demonstrable loss and presumed psychological indignity that itself sometimes rests on interpretive assumptions about how particular statements will tend to resonate with recipients and thus affect the plaintiff.

The common law's strict liability standard and the attendant system of awarding damages have, however, been gradually softened over the years by the creation of constitutional defenses against defamation claims. In the 1964 *NY Times v. Sullivan* case, which involved a libel judgment imposed by an Alabama trial court for minor factual mistakes in an editorial advertisement decrying the treatment of civil rights protesters by the Montgomery police, the Court in *Sullivan* formally applied constitutional protection to libelous statements for the first time. As Justice Brennan reasoned in the majority opinion, too unforgiving a standard for defamation creates chilling effects because some speakers will judge it too costly to risk liability for incidental inaccuracies or caustic statements that fell into ambiguous territory between fact and opinion. Public discourse overall would suffer, as the roster of participants and the vehemence with which they participate would be enervated.[7] Recovery for defamation would only be allowed for a public official like Police Commissioner Sullivan if they could prove that the false statements were made either deliberately or so recklessly that they flagrantly flouted the conventions of ordinary journalistic due diligence. They called this the "actual malice" standard. It was particularly important to encourage robust discussion about public officials like Sullivan, according to the logic of the standard, and thus the rules had to ensure that speakers would participate freely enough to make the public conversation "uninhibited, robust, and wide-open."

In a theoretical sense, the *Sullivan* case and subsequent revisions of the constitutional limitations on defamation law were therefore grounded in what is usually described as the "marketplace" theory of free speech. The seminal articulation of this framework in the larger context of a theory of liberalism comes from philosopher John Stuart Mill's mid-nineteenth century work *On Liberty*.[8] In this framework, the goal of any legal guarantee of freedom of expression is to encourage the greatest volume of speech so that ideas can compete with one another in the search for truth. This includes speech about government and the affairs of the state – what the Supreme Court calls "political speech" – but also discussion of social and even mundane interpersonal issues that help us to coordinate our lives and make judgments about those around us, and commercial information that helps us to make consumer decisions.[9] The marketplace perspective assumes, following Mill, that the only speech worth curtailing would be directly injurious (and therefore sanctionable under the "harm principle") or that which is factually false. Otherwise, in a phrase that has become somewhat of a cliche, the marketplace theory contends that the remedy for "bad" speech is *more* speech.[10]

The decision in *Sullivan* was thus emblematic of the vision for the First Amendment that prioritizes maximizing the range of viewpoints available to the public to invigorate the marketplace of ideas. More specifically, though, the ultimate goal of protecting speech is not simply to defend the liberty of the speaker; following philosopher Alexander Meiklejohn's "town meeting" analogy for free speech protection, it is to make sure that the public discourse is enriched for *listeners*. As legal scholar Harry Kalven and others have pointed out, the *Sullivan* opinion evinced a particular vision in which the purpose of the First Amendment is to encourage the citizen critic of government for the benefit of all observers, not just for the liberty interests of the speaker.[11]

The *Sullivan* case also captures how the core tenets of modern libel law were shaped in response to the prevailing media environment of the time, and thus provides a kind of counterpoint to the digital age. It is widely remarked that the civil rights context created the real urgency for the Court to curtail the common law rules because southern officials were using them to effectively shut down national coverage of civil rights struggles in the south.[12] The presumption, then, was that wider public awareness of these issues hinged significantly on the fate of a few publications.

Further, the circumstances surrounding the publication of the statements were more or less transparent. The speakers were in no way mysterious, as the organization responsible for running the ad had signed its name and made its address available to receive donations. There were a handful of editors at the paper to whom police commissioner Sullivan could appeal directly for a retraction (he was refused). While there was some argument over whether the ad would be understood to refer to Sullivan in the first place, it was easy to figure out roughly how many people would have been exposed to the ad based on how many copies of the paper circulated in Alabama (not many, though this hardly mattered in a case of libel per se). Finally, it was easy to see that Sullivan was by basically any definition a public official for all purposes and thus would be subject to the new actual malice rule. He may have sought vindication through a libel lawsuit, but he could just as easily have commanded the public's attention through publicity endeavors of his own. The relative ease of apprehending these variables thus makes the case a paradigmatic reputational dispute for a public sphere dominated by mass media.

Following *Sullivan*, the question of exactly which plaintiffs should be subject to the "actual malice" standard took center stage. In *Gertz v. Welch* (1974), the Court attempted to resolve nearly a decade of oscillation on this question, determining that it applied only to public officials and certain categories of what the Court called public figures (like celebrities or people who are prominent in the discussion of some particular issue), and that any defamation plaintiff had to determine that statements were made at least negligently, i.e. having disregarded ordinary due diligence.[13] In dicta, however, Justice Powell additionally articulated the underlying spirit of the Court's approach to libel law: "the first remedy of any victim of defamation is self-help – using available opportunities to contradict the lie or correct the error, and thereby to minimize its adverse impact on reputation."[14] While the actual legal test does not technically require plaintiffs to show that they tried to pursue self-help first, the availability of self-help (or "access to the means of corrective counterspeech") is a factor weighed in determining whether a plaintiff is a public or private figure as a matter of law. This principle that self-help is the preferred first resort when someone feels their reputation has been unduly maligned thus introduces an important variable into any consideration of how to balance speech and reputation protection: what means exist by which the victim can try to vindicate him or herself?

American tort law also seeks to balance speech and reputation protection when speech is thought to harm the reputation of a business. Even before the *Sullivan* case, courts had recognized the closely related tort of commercial disparagement. In a commercial disparagement, the injury being recognized is more squarely financial in nature, but the conceptual essence is similar: statements that were made in order to harm the way a business or its products are thought about and which were made either recklessly or with knowledge of their falsehood.[15] The balance that must be struck is likewise similar to that contemplated in ordinary defamation law. Just as it is important to subject the conduct of individuals (especially those who command inordinate public attention or trust) to discussion that is "uninhibited, robust, and wide-open," there is also substantial social value in protecting citizens' ability to share opinions and voice complaints about commercial entities. In fact, the Supreme Court directly recognized that the First Amendment applied to commercial information in addition to more politically oriented speech in the 1976 *Virginia Pharmacy* case (which, while it concerned regulations on advertising specifically, essentially declared commercial speech to be protected under the First Amendment). The majority opinion by Justice Harry Blackmun reasoned that "as long as we preserve a predominantly free enterprise economy, the allocation of our resources in large measure will be made through numerous private economic decisions." Because of this, it therefore "is a matter of public interest that those decisions, in the aggregate, be intelligent and well informed," a goal for which "the free flow of commercial information is indispensable."[16]

Finally, the law also provides limited redress for speech or information disclosure that falls under the somewhat amorphous category of "invasion of privacy." The legal recognition of a need to recognize such invasion as a civil injury is generally traceable to Samuel Warren and Louis D. Brandeis' seminal "Right to Privacy" article from 1890, in which they proposed that tort law should rectify "public disclosure in the press of truthful but private details about the individual which caused emotional upset to him."[17] A version of the Warren and Brandeis concept had been embraced in many jurisdictions by the early 1960s, when law professor William Prosser outlined the four related but distinct invasion of privacy torts that were being recognized by courts across the country: public disclosure of private facts, false light, intrusion upon seclusion, and misappropriation of likeness. This typology is codified today in the Restatement of Torts.

While false light is similar to defamation and misappropriation is a conceptual cousin of intellectual property, the tort of "public disclosure of private facts" concerns an aspect of reputation not captured in defamation law: information that is true but highly personal and perhaps embarrassing. While varying from state to state, the tort of public disclosure of private facts has two core components: the information at issue must be sufficiently "private" – meaning information "which the ordinary person would find highly personal and the disclosure of which would offend a person of ordinary sensibilities" – and it must be disseminated widely. Such disclosures may be protected from liability if they are deemed "newsworthy."

Since the creation of constitutional protections for some categories of libelous statements and the general recognition of the privacy torts across jurisdictions, courts and legal scholars have also tried to better understand what exactly it is that plaintiffs seek to achieve in bringing defamation and invasion of privacy actions. This query operates in a similar spirit to Justice Powell's counseling of self-help when available: if winning money damages is not the primary motivation, then perhaps alternative methods of resolution could secure a feeling of "justice" in place of the traditional defamation lawsuit.

Randall P. Bezanson developed one of the more comprehensive studies of plaintiff motivations. In an influential 1986 article, Bezanson wrote that "the principal object of the lawsuit for most plaintiffs is not to obtain monetary relief for financial harm." Instead, the major motivating factors are restoring reputation, correcting what plaintiffs view as falsity, and vengeance.[18] Going to court can be gratifying for plaintiffs, but this is because it happens to be the most visible and symbolically important means of speaking up for oneself, not because it is inherently the most useful:

> To [plaintiffs], the libel suit represents an official engagement of the judicial system on their behalf, and the act of suing represents a legitimation of their claims of falsehood. Indeed, *many plaintiffs may believe they have no other means of recourse*, and therefore feel that litigation is the only way to set the record straight (italics added).[19]

This perhaps explains the attractiveness of libel suits despite the low success rate, which at the time was found to be between 5% and 10% in cases involving media defendants.[20]

The idea that what plaintiffs truly want is public exoneration (perhaps coupled with shaming of the alleged defamer) achieved through a visible and official determination of truth or falsity was encouraging for reform. In this vein, Rodney Smolla and other libel reform advocates pushed to multiply the hurdles that plaintiffs would have to clear in order to proceed to a trial. Instead, such proposals substituted more opportunities to effectively settle the dispute through negotiation with the speaker for public correction or through a declaratory judgment from a court on the issue of truth or falsity alone. First, as Smolla wrote, it was important to come to terms with the fact that "the traditional suit for money damages has proven an exceptionally poor vehicle for meaningful reputational redress," and this is because

> they tend to drag on interminably, are enormously costly for both sides, and very rarely end in a clear-cut resolution of what ought to be the heart of the matter: a determination of the truth or falsity of what was published.[21]

In response, Smolla advanced a libel reform proposal in the mid-1980s that sought to redirect the machinery of defamation law toward this kind of efficient correction of the record and away from arduous jury trials. Smolla proposed a three-pronged approach focusing on the core factual resolution that should, after all, be the crux of the average reputational dispute. The first prong was a "forceful retraction and reply mechanism" that would preclude a lawsuit when executed within particular parameters; the second was a declaratory judgment action to decide whether the statement in question is true or false if the defendant fails to honor either the request for reply or retraction; and, finally, a suit for damages would be available in the event that both of these options fail, though only actual damages would be recoverable.[22] Smolla's group failed to dramatically overhaul libel law, but the proposal sparked a substantive conversation about various methods of delivering "justice" in a reputational dispute and arguably helped to catalyze the creation of statutory retraction mechanisms in several states.[23]

To the extent that they encourage collaboration between parties and public negotiation of the issues in question (even if it is conducted in an acrimonious fashion), self-help frameworks and reforms emphasizing rebuttal and retraction can perhaps be justified in terms of their overall social benefit. In this manner, they implicate the legal theory concept of "private ordering," or the "sharing of regulatory authority with private actors" who resolve disputes based on a set of shared norms.[24] Such private ordering is sometimes thought to be publicly beneficial in ways that legal dispute resolution is not. In the context of regulating reputationally consequent speech, this is visible if we consider the value that has been attached to such scenarios by the legal scholars Vincent Blasi and Donald Downs.

Blasi sees the resolution of reputational disputes through social rather than purely legal channels as a means of enhancing the legitimacy of the resulting sanctions and the behavioral limits they reinforce. If these limits evolve organically through social mechanisms like approval, confrontation, and shaming, he reasons, then they are more likely to become widely accepted. He asserts this by invoking Milton's characterization of the power of social resolutions via unfettered confrontation: "[i]nformal, nonofficial sanctions and judgments," Milton recognized, "will always provide the most important 'bonds and ligaments that hold a society together." He likewise advanced a conception of redress redolent of the marketplace theory: "[Those] who assault the sensibilities of the public will be reined in when their tactics cause audiences to recoil and their opponents to succeed in discrediting them."[25] Richard Epstein also positions these "bonds and ligaments" as ancillary enforcers of standards of conduct even within developed legal systems. As he writes,

> [t]he basic rules of primary conduct (i.e., those that arose naturally to regulate conduct between ordinary individuals without interference from the law) that arose in a regime of pure self-help offer the best structure for individual rights and duties even after the creation of a viable public force.

The law, in this view, should therefore encourage such direct social negotiation when possible.

This free speech ethos can in turn help instill in the citizen a kind of social fortitude and willingness to confront and question the attitudes and ideas that one encounters – or what Blasi calls "good character." For Blasi, this is an integral component of democratic citizenship: "a culture that prizes and protects expressive liberty nurtures in its members certain character traits such as inquisitiveness, independence of judgment, distrust of authority, willingness to take initiative, perseverance, and the courage to confront evil."[26] In the context of disputes over statements that affect reputation, some degree of confrontation can thus be seen as positive: "The resulting environment, in which dissent is both an option and an inescapable reality, is the principal source of the characterological effect."[27]

For Donald Downs, the concept of "republican virtue" describes a related value: that it is important in a democracy for communities to be self-reliant in managing problems and confronting problematic forces within their own ranks. Because of our republican form of democratic representation and the corresponding need for citizens to play an active role in pursuing the priorities and values of their communities, it is critical for citizens to engage one another in dialogue and confront the difficult social choices about which they must deliberate rather than shirking them. The emphasis on deliberation and confrontation in the marketplace theory of free speech is implicitly directed toward promulgating republican virtue.[28] Likewise, the priorities of the republican virtue framework resonate with Blasi's notion that confrontation with and protection of dissent encourages the "good character" that a democratic citizenry must develop.

While it might seem counterintuitive, the notion of pluralistic confrontation in the marketplace of ideas having a salutary civic impact also infuses the conception of the public interest found in theories of ethical public relations advocacy. Thomas Bivins has framed the issue in terms of contribution to public debate, arguing that

> if public relations as a profession improves the quality of debate over issues important to the public, then the public interest will be served…[b]y providing voices for special interests, public relations contributes to the harmonization of diverse points of view.[29]

James Grunig likewise argues that "[h]ow well public relations adds value to marketplaces and public policy arenas will justify its status as a profession." Specifically, the profession adds to these arenas when open dialogue gives people an opportunity to participate in as well as witness discussions (statements and counter statements) by which customers (markets) and publics (stakeholders/stakeseekers [sic]) have the opportunity to examine facts, values, policies, identifications, and narratives leading to wiser purchases as well as more sound public policies.[30]

Kathy Fitzpatrick has gone further toward explicitly situating public relations ethics within the conceptual coordinates of the marketplace of ideas and free speech theory. She describes how public relations scholar Scott Cutlip, for instance, has framed the "social justification for public relations" in terms of its contribution to the marketplace of ideas, as practitioners "plead the case of a client or organization in the free-wheeling forum of debate."[31] Martin and Wright likewise note how public relations legend John Hill (of the firm Hill & Knowlton) adopted a similar marketplace-oriented perspective, likening the practice of public relations to advocacy in a courtroom: "let the litigants present their cases and let the public decide whose arguments carry the day, just as in a court of law."[32]

In fact, Fitzpatrick writes, professional public relations organizations have themselves embraced the spirit of this marketplace-oriented approach: "core concepts of advocacy in the PRSA Code of Ethics reflect democratic ideals grounded in First Amendment legal theory" (p. 1). This is manifest specifically in the Code's statement that "[p]rotecting and advancing the free flow of accurate and truthful information is essential to serving the public interest and contributing to informed decision making in a democratic society" (p. 1). In order to do so, practitioners should be mindful of "whether public relations advocacy helps equalize access to the marketplace or, rather, creates an imbalance of power in the marketplace is an important issue in determining the limits of responsible advocacy."[33] If the practice of public relations is "intended to monopolize the marketplace and freeze out other voices" then it "violate[s] fundamental democratic principles."[34]

These characterizations thus resonate with the spirit of the marketplace of ideas justification for free speech protection and the concerns about overzealous reputation defense voiced in debates over the proper contours of defamation and privacy law: in advocating for clients, public relations practitioners theoretically enhance the search for truth rather than distort it. While this notion is directly relevant in a professional sense for the practitioners of reputation management whom we will meet in later chapters, its introduction here is also intended to establish that the values associated with the marketplace of ideas concept and free speech in general can be applied beyond the legal realm in a conceptual sense: we can evaluate whether particular practices or attitudes might contribute to or undermine a robust and diverse public discourse even if they are not backed by legal mandate per se.

Conclusion

This overview of the relationships between the marketplace of ideas concept and both the legal regulation of reputation and the forms of "private ordering" that complement it has intended to establish the core conceptual variables that come into play in any discussion of the conflict between free speech and protection from undue reputational harm. Reputational harm includes both material and psychological dimensions, and it is important that societies provide redress for those who have been unduly maligned or humiliated. Yet there is also a danger of this redress being too extensive and threatening the "uninhibited, robust, and wide-open" public discourse that is critical for a flourishing "marketplace of ideas" – the benefit of which is incurred by *listeners* as well as speakers. To this end, the courts have been particularly circumspect about imposing liability for true statements, though the privacy torts do offer relief in limited circumstances. And even though they are not state actors obligated to follow the First Amendment, public relations experts have also developed a kind of conceptual consensus in the "public interest" orientation of PR that conceives of responsible, ethical public relations practice as adding to rather than subtracting from or distorting the "marketplace of ideas."

The relationship between legal redress and private action in combating reputationally damaging speech also must be assessed based on the individual person and the subject matter being spoken about: how important is it that the information is known, to how wide an audience, does the person being spoken about have the means of responding with effective "counterspeech," and could alternative forms of resolution perhaps more efficiently or directly provide the plaintiff with the vindication that they seek? If the latter is possible, the logic goes, then perhaps this represents the best possible avenue to pursue, as it avoids the costly and slow-moving machinery of the state, adds to rather than subtracts from the marketplace of ideas, and can increase perceptions of social legitimacy and feelings of personal and community empowerment. It is specifically these kinds of alternative "private ordering" approaches to reputational disputes, in fact, that will move to the foreground in the contemporary debates around online speech and reputation management.

Notes

1 John Whitfield, *People will Talk: The Surprising Science of Reputation.* Hoboken, NJ: Wiley (2011), 5.
2 John C. Martin, "The Role of Retraction in Defamation Suits." *University of Chicago Law Review* 1993.1 (1993), 304.
3 Chris Komisarjevsky, *The Power of Reputation.* New York: AMACOM Publishing (2012).
4 Gloria Origgi et al., *Reputation: What It Is and Why It Matters.* Princeton: Princeton University Press (2017), 171.
5 See Lior Jacob Strahilovitz, "Less Regulation, More Reputation." In Hassan Masum and Mark Tovey (Eds.), *The Reputation Society.* Cambridge, MA: MIT Press (2011), 66–67.
6 Here is the characterization, for instance, of the kinds of harms that fit the category of presumed damages – or damages that are assumed from the nature of the statement – in Illinois law: "presumed damages are defined as personal humiliation, embarrassment, injury to reputation and standing in the community, mental suffering, and anguish and anxiety." [#] That list thus includes five terms that describe feelings or psychological states compared to just the one material factor of "standing in the community." Charles E. Harris II, "Even Presumed Damages Must be Proven," 2. https://www.mayerbrown.com/Files/Publication/1d08db7c-5380-475a-9ce4-e780095606a6/Presentation/PublicationAttachment/17af5d1b-5fa0-4ebe-b45c-df4c11147287/ARTICLE-Harris_Presumed_Damages_0810.pdf.
7 Justice Brennan's opinion drew on James Madison's notion that "some abuse is inseparable from the proper use of everything; and in no instance is this more true than in that of the press" in order to argue (citing *NAACP v. Button*) that "erroneous statement is inevitable in free debate, and that it must be protected if the freedoms of expression are to have the 'breathing space' that they 'need...to survive.'" 376 U.S. 254, 272.
8 The following gloss is derived from Mill, *On Liberty*, Chs. 1 and 2.
9 As Justice Black wrote in *Mills v. Alabama*, "Whatever differences may exist about interpretations of the First Amendment, there is practically universal agreement that a major purpose of that Amendment was to protect the free discussion of governmental affairs." *Mills v. Alabama*, 384 U.S. 214 (1966).
Excluding its slanderous and libelous forms, of course, sociologists have contended that gossip can in fact play a pro-social function in a modern liberal democracy. As the synopsis of one book on the subject explains, "[p]eople gossip about the rich and famous in order to 'cut them down to size,' and informal gossip networks help overcome the depersonalizing tendencies of modern society." Robert F. Goodman and Aaron Ben-Ze'ev (Eds.), *Good Gossip.* Lawrence: University of Kansas Press (1994). https://kansaspress.ku.edu/978-0-7006-0670-2.html.
Finally, the Supreme Court has recognized that commercial speech is protected by the First Amendment. See *Virginia State Pharmacy Board v. Virginia Citizens Consumer Council*, 425 U.S. 748 (1976).
10 The seminal expression of this idea actually comes not from Mill directly, but from Justice Brandeis' influential concurring opinion in *Whitney v California*, in which he wrote: "If there be time to expose through discussion,

the falsehoods and fallacies, to avert the evil by the processes of education, the remedy to be applied is more speech, not enforced silence." *Whitney v. California*, 274 U.S. 357 (1927).

11 Harry Kalven, *A Worthy Tradition: Freedom of Speech in America*. New York: Harper Collins (1988), 209.

12 See Kermit Hall and Melvin Urofsky, *New York Times v. Sullivan: Civil Rights, Libel Law, and the Free Press*. Lawrence: University Press of Kansas (2011), 182.

13 In the following years there was yet more debate about who exactly constituted a public figure, with the courts eventually settling on a test similar to that from *Gertz* in *Waldbaum v. Fairchild Publications* (1980). The D.C. Circuit clarified that a plaintiff was a limited-purpose public figure (the category of public figure that had caused the most debate) if he or she had or sought "a major impact on the resolution of a specific public dispute that has foreseeable and substantial ramifications for persons beyond its immediate participants." 27 F.2d 1287 (D.C. Cir.), cert. denied.

14 *Gertz*, 418 U.S. 346.

15 See the following overview: https://www.findlaw.com/smallbusiness/business-laws-and-regulations/commercial-disparagement.html.

16 *Virginia State Board of Pharmacy v. Virginia Citizens Consumer Council, Inc.*, 425 U.S. 748 (1976), 765.

17 Samuel Warren and Louis D. Brandeis, "The Right to Privacy." *Harvard Law Review* 4 (Dec. 15, 1890), 193.

18 Randall Bezanson, "The Libel Suit in Retrospect: What Plaintiffs Want and What Plaintiffs Get." *California Law Review* 74.3 (1986), 791.

19 Bezanson, "Libel Suit," 791.

20 Kathy Roberts Forde, *Literary Journalism on Trial: Masson V. New Yorker and the First Amendment*. Amherst: University of Massachusetts Press (2008), 122–23.

21 Rodney Smolla, "The Annenberg Libel Reform Proposal: The Case for Enactment," *William and Mary Law Review* 31.1 (1989), 45, 31.

22 Smolla, "Annenberg Proposal," 32–34.

23 As the Digital Media Law Project explains, "A growing number of states have laws – both statutory and case law – that require that a plaintiff must first request a retraction before they can recover certain types of damages in a defamation lawsuit." A list of statutes by state with descriptions is available here: http://www.dmlp.org/legal-guide/state-law-retractions.

24 Schwarcz in fact categorizes this as only one of several types of private ordering, but it is the one that is most relevant to this kind of dispute resolution. To illustrate the principle, he cites The seminal work on Robert Ellickson's "study of the interaction of cattlemen in Shasta County, California. [Ellickson] observes that this community of cattlemen had generated a set of private norms that, he argues, maximizes the general welfare of the group, without government intervention." Schwarcz, "Private Ordering," 7–8.

25 David Koehler, "Self Help, the Media, and the First Amendment." *Hofstra Law Review* 35 (2007), 1284.

26 Vincent Blasi, "Free Speech and Good Character," 46 UCLA L. Rev. 1567–1582 (1999), 1569.

27 Blasi, "Good Character," 1569, 1572.

28 For an example, Downs describes how certain participants in the infamous "Nazis in Skokie" conflict (in which a neo-nazi organization threatened, but then eventually declined, to march through the village of Skokie, IL – home to a number of holocaust survivors) described its ultimately positive outcome in terms of republican virtue. For instance, an ACLU lawyer argued that "[t]he best consequence of the Nazis' proposal to march in Skokie is that it produced more speech…[i]t stimulated more discussion of the evils of Nazism." Perhaps more importantly, republican virtue can be seen as a product of the direct confrontation between the survivors and the NSPA: because survivors often described how the conflict had brought them together to be "strong" rather than "silent," Downs argues that the public response of the community to unify in resistance to Collin and the NSPA produced "ends commensurate with the republican virtue function of free speech." Donald Downs, *Nazis in Skokie: Freedom, Community, and the First Amendment*. South Bend, IN: Notre Dame University Press (1985), 112.

29 Kathy Fitzpatrick and Candace Gauthier, "Toward a Professional Responsibility Theory of Public Relations Ethics." *Journal of Mass Media Ethics* 16.2–3 (2001), 204.

30 James E. Grunig, "Two-Way Symmetrical Public Relations." In Robert Heath (Ed.), *The Handbook of Public Relations*. Thousand Oaks, CA: Sage (2001), 85–86.

31 Kathy Fitzpatrick, "Baselines for Ethical Advocacy in the 'Marketplace of Ideas.'" In Kathy Fitzpatrick and Carolyn Bronstein (Eds.), *Ethics in Public Relations*. Thousand Oaks, CA: Sage (2006), 3, 1–17.

32 Dick Martin and Donald Wright, *Public Relations Ethics: How to Practice Pr without Losing Your Soul*. New York: Business Expert Press (2016), 122.

33 Fitzpatrick, "Baselines for Ethical Advocacy," 9.

34 Fitzpatrick, "Baselines for Ethical Advocacy," 9.

2 Reputational Precarity in the Digital Age

This chapter covers major perspectives on how the internet has altered the coordinates by which reputations are constructed, maintained, and assessed. To construct this portrait, it looks to two central sources of commentary: the analytical and, at times, critical assessments of digital media and legal scholars, and the more practically oriented assessments and advice of the business commentariat and reputation management professionals, who ultimately articulate a vision of the ethos necessary to thrive in this environment.

The voices in this chapter largely identify three central components of how reputation works differently in the digital age. The first of these is that the scope and visibility of information on the web creates more enduring, indelible reputational threats – whether from malicious gossip, deliberate lies, or true but unflattering information. This is complemented by the second component, the conflation of personal and professional activity on digital media platforms in the construction of reputation. Discussions of reputation in this register suggest that there is no "private" zone of mediated activity that can be separated from a person's professional life or between the person's social domains. Third, we see from both critical observations of scholars and the advice offered by professionals and industry observers that both the architecture of digital platforms and the accompanying dynamics of human information processing produce an environment in which individuals are likely to be assessed ungenerously – either deliberately or as a largely unconscious adaptation to information overload. Taken together, these features undergird an ethos that is consistently articulated in reputation management discourse: while the threats may be legion, the machinery of online reputation can be harnessed to our advantage, and we face a new kind of self-help imperative to take control of our reputations through constant monitoring and strategic self-presentation.

DOI: 10.4324/9781003287384-3

The Construction and Scrutiny of Digital Identities

Siva Vaidhyanathan has provided a useful framework for characteriz-ing what is novel about reputational concerns in the digital age. Specif-ically, Vaidhyanathan argues that an individual is subject to increased public scrutiny in the digital environment: he calls this the "person to public" interface of the web. In Vaidhyanathan's telling, the affor-dances of the web for connection and discovery also result in greater personal exposure. As he writes,

[a]t this interface, which is now located largely online, people have found their lives exposed, their names and faces ridiculed, and their well-being harmed immeasurably by the rapid proliferation of images, the asocial nature of much ostensibly 'social' web be-havior, and the permanence of the digital record.[1]

LinkedIn founder Reid Hoffman has thus argued that in the contem-porary "networked age...everything becomes a reputational issue...[it] is a major component to everything—relationships, decision making and so on."[2]

To be sure, concern about scrutiny of one's image is not unique to the internet. People have been ridiculed and gossiped about in schools, on playing fields, at work, and in both private correspondence and the print and broadcast media for a long time. More specifically, then, the novelty of the contemporary situation resides first in the way in which the internet is used has broken down boundaries that we used to enjoy between different social and informational domains. Vaidhyanathan characterizes the difference this way: "Whereas in our real social lives we have learned to manage our reputations, the online environments in which we work and play have broken down the barriers that separate the different social contexts in which we move."[3] The consequence, ul-timately, is a kind of integration of both experience and informational revelation that erases the distinction between different social spheres.

Vaidhyanathan's formulation informs the more specific notion of "context collapse" in digital media advanced by Alice Marwick and danah boyd [sic].[4] This is the idea that the architecture and conven-tions of such platforms make it difficult to maintain a boundary be-tween the distinct styles of context-appropriate self-presentation that are characteristic of face-to-face interaction. This collapse is manifest specifically as an erosion of the distinction between professional and personal reputation, and in the case of search engine results, it might be relatively meaningless to distinguish between information related to one's professional endeavors and one's personal life. Further, as Reputation Defender founder Michael Fertik points out, one's personal reputation can also become inextricably linked with the reputation of a business.[5] As Marwick and boyd assert, correspondingly, those who participate in social platforms therefore "learn that 'successful' social media use requires self-monitoring and censorship — one must always be mindful of the internet audience."[6] Yet no matter our efforts, according to Vaidhyanathan, the overall impact of existing within this digital media environment is that "we cede more and more control over our reputations every day."[7]

Ilana Gershon's research on job-seeking and hiring provides additional insight into the ways in which the information visible through search and social media is used to assess individuals, and in turn, how this conditions our own subjectivities. The platform LinkedIn epitomizes the difficulty of representing oneself in this paradigm of what Gershon calls the "self-as-business" that blurs the personal and the professional online. A LinkedIn page represents "a marketing document in which you can present yourself as a bundle of unweighted skills (endorsements), unweighted relationships (connections), and experiences," she writes, and as a result, "the LinkedIn version of the self-as-business consistently errs on the side of being context-free."[8]

In her interviews with hiring managers, she found that it was instead often "second-order" information that was being used to assess candidates as much as more holistic, narrative-oriented "first-order" information like a candidate's background or demonstrable skills. She writes that she

> came across plenty of other instances in which hiring managers or HR managers admitted that they screened people for how they used media to communicate. One woman in HR told me that she would check people's Facebook profiles regularly to see how they presented themselves.

Importantly, the information being sought was not merely about the applicant's behavior per se, as the hiring manager told her that "[s]he did not care whether they drank alcohol, but she did think twice if she saw too many photographs of the person drinking." In other words, the "information" being observed was a

> glimpse into the kinds of social judgment this person exhibited[,] and [if] she saw Facebook photographs of a person drinking or wearing risque clothes as a warning sign that he or she might behave indiscreetly in other contexts as well.[9]

The screening of this kind of personal activity in the employment context is also often characterized by a "weed out" mentality according to Gershon. A hiring manager that Gershon interviewed acknowledged that "he was not reading resumes in a generous light, or trying to see the potential in every candidate" when he screened applicants. Out of what he perceived as necessity, "[i]nstead, he was primarily reading to say no – and these noes often depended on quick judgments about how people represented themselves based on relatively little information."[10] Seemingly trivial details in a candidate's self-presentation online can be the basis for one of these "noes." Kristi Piehl, the CEO of a public relations firm called Media Minefield, describes an instance where she "Googled a potential employee and came across her LinkedIn profile," and "nearly didn't hire her...because there was a grammatical error on it." "This," Piehl emphasizes, "is why your online brand matters."[11]

The "mistaken online identity" phenomenon is also popularly invoked as a reputational danger for job seekers in the digital age. The website job-hunt.org, which is published by a longtime human resource professional and consultant named Susan Joyce and provides extensive advice to applicants and insight into hiring practices, offers a digital age parable in which "Mary #1," a well-qualified job-seeker who has led a "blameless life," is sabotaged unwittingly by "Mary #2," a "disbarred attorney [with the same first and last name] living in the same state as Mary #1."[12] The upshot, according to Joyce, is that like Gershon's interviewee above, this can be enough to sink a candidate when so many employers are "reading to say no." "Employers these days don't have the time – *or the need* – to determine if the bad stuff they have found is about the applicant they are considering," she cautions; "[t]hey just move on to the next applicant, and discard your application."[13] This assumption is echoed in an advertisement for an Austin, TX based reputation management service, which warns the proactive attention to the digital impression one makes is essential, as "you aren't hearing even a tiniest fraction of the negative fallout and consequences [from a suboptimal image]." This is because "no one tells you those; they form an impression and simply move on to the next suitors/suitresses, candidate/candidates, etc."[14]

Adjacently, law professor Daniel Solove has analyzed the restructuring of gossip online in terms of the way in which context is stripped out of digital identities. "Before the internet," Solove writes, "gossip would spread by word of mouth and remain within the boundaries of the social circle."[15] The issue for Solove is not the fact that the social circle is effectively wider on the internet; it is that the interpretive dynamics of the social circle change when discrete bits of information are encountered by strangers who have no overall contextual knowledge of the subject of the statements. As he puts it, "[i]n the small village...disreputable information would be judged within the context of a person's entire life," whereas just as Gershon's interviewees emphasized regarding the decontextualized assessment of candidates, Solove argues that "[n]ow, people are judged out of context based on information fragments found online."[16] In other words, the structure of information exchange and discovery on the internet makes it more likely that searchers will be either unable or unlikely to understand the figurative asterisks that may otherwise accompany a particular statement or description. Solove sees this as a central informational feature of "generation Google."[17]

Further, Solove sees a qualitative difference in the reputational consequences of online speech. This is due to the relative permanence of content on the web that is not deliberately deleted or otherwise rendered less visible through changes in search engine indexing. Michael Fertik echoes this characterization of the information architecture of the internet affects reputation construction: companies like Google have made everything findable very quickly, and inexpensive storage (e.g. via Amazon Cloud) means that it is effectively cheaper to store than to expend the effort to delete.[18] Solove goes on to contrast the social world prior to the internet in which "[g]ossip used to travel in local circles...and would be forgotten with time" with the digital networks on which "gossip is no longer ephemeral."[19] The contrast is the same with the social practice of shaming, as it was "once localized and fleeting, [but] shaming online creates a permanent record of people's past transgressions — a digital scarlet letter."[20] Such a characterization may sound hyperbolic, but it is understandable if we consider the way in which search engine links indexed to a person's name can play such a profound role in dictating (and some would argue distorting) the public informational profile for that person.

These dynamics can increase the scale and permanence of shaming exponentially. As Fertik characterizes the situation, "[t]he most obvious result of this revolution in digital storage is that blemishes on your reputation will live on indefinitely." He offers some hypothetical scenarios to illustrate the magnitude:

> Even a one-time mistake will follow you forever if it takes place in the digital realm — and what doesn't these days? Did a video of you snapping at a customer during your worst day end up on YouTube? Did you get caught reviewing your own business? Or did a nosy neighbor with Google Glass catch you enjoying a candlelit dinner

with a stranger while your husband was on a business trip — and post a picture of it to Facebook?

After observing this phenomenon in action, British Journalist Jon Ronson has endeavored to re-humanize some of the targets of viral criticism online, arguing that their "public shaming" creates situations in which we "refuse to let them back into the world."[21] Perspectives like Fertik's and Ronson's suggest that absent some kind of informational intervention, those targeted in this manner are permanently tarnished; their Google results have led to them being ostracized.

The persistence of digital memory is further compounded by the architecture of social media applications generally and by their omnipresence in the lives of young people. Media scholar Kate Eichhorn has argued that digital media has ushered in the "end of forgetting." Though her book of the same name is primarily focused on the experiences of children and teens, the phenomenon that she describes is nonetheless increasingly widespread, as more and more people grow up in a situation where they "carry forward...not simply an archive of digital images and video clips but an entire social context that they may or may not wish to retain."[22] The journalist Lauren Goode has provided a stark example of how the architecture of the social web is in fact designed to perpetually remind us of earlier moments in our digitally mediated lives, thus flattening the distinction between past and present social contexts. In a 2021 *Wired* article, she reflects on the experience of breaking off an engagement years prior and still being bombarded with "memory" reminders from the various applications she had used to document the time in her life as they neared the wedding. Goode describes how her "sense of time and place bec[ame] warped... when algorithms surface[d] these images," likening it to being haunted by "a cyborg version of me, a digital ghost, that is still getting married" while instead "[t]he real me would really like to move on now."[23]

Vaidhyanathan provides another critical scholarly perspective on the ways in which the structure of digital reputation construction impedes personal reinvention. Unlike in the 1920s, when F. Scott Fitzgerald's titular character Gatsby could disavow his humble origins, Vaidhanathan argues figuratively that "Jay Gatsby could not exist today...[because t]he digital ghost of Jay Gatz would follow him everywhere." The general takeaway, for Vaidhanathan, is thus that "there are no second acts, or second chances, in the digital age."[24] He singles out search engines specifically as the factor that has removed "substantial autonomy and control over one's record." While Fitzgerald's Gatsby may not be the most sympathetic example in this regard, the more general upshot for ordinary people is that "as long as our past indiscretions can be easily Googled by potential employers or U.S. security agents," he therefore concludes, "our social, intellectual, and actual mobility is limited."[25]

The marketing professional Kale Sligh adds credence to this idea from a professional perspective. He has concluded from his experience over the years that it is "scary" how

> [n]o longer can you get in trouble or do something dumb (we've all been there), learn from it and move on…[because t]he Internet most often is permanent, and those stupid decisions can follow you for the rest of your life.[26]

Or, as Ronson puts it more pithily, the tendency is for the digital identity constructed in search results to "reduc[e] [a person] to the worst thing they ever did."[27]

Or didn't even do. The rise of "deepfake" technology – which tech journalist Nina Schick defines as "synthetic media…that is used maliciously" in her book on the subject, has added a further wrinkle to the digital information environment.[28] Deepfakes can be used to "make people say things they never said and do things they never did," such as the infamous video in which an AI-synthezied image of "Barack Obama" (created by filmmaker Jordan Peele as a cautionary example of the power of the technology) warns that we must become more vigilant about what we trust on the internet or else risk becoming a "fucked up dystopia."[29] While Schick and others rightly focus much attention on the way in which this increasingly ubiquitous technology threatens to undermine political debate by destroying any possible consensus about the set of facts upon which debate is based, they also highlight some of the ways in which synthetic media can be used maliciously to besmirch an individual's reputation. Legal scholar Danielle Citron, for instance, has characterized how the use of deepfake technology to create synthetic pornography has both an emotional and informational impact. She describes the situation in the following way:

> Deepfake technology is being weaponized against women by inserting their faces into porn. It is terrifying, embarrassing, demeaning, and silencing. Deepfake sex videos say to individuals that their bodies are not their own and can make it difficult to stay online, get or keep a job, and feel safe.[30]

Others have reinforced this idea that even outside of situations involving outright disinformation, the composition of results in search engines tends to reinforce reductive, incendiary, or simply inaccurate portraits of individual human beings. As legal scholar Brian Leiter has argued, Google's search results algorithm elevates speech that may be the most controversial or in some way linked to highly trafficked sites but that hardly seems like the most relevant or reliable profile of a person in any informational sense. As he puts it (referring to the case of AutoAdmit, a prominent law school message board that became dominated by virulently sexist and racist flaming), "the idea that the 'most relevant and reliable results' about a female student at Yale law school consist of the anonymous rantings of misogynistic sociopaths would be amusing if real people were not involved."[31] Similarly, Solove dismisses the idea that the proliferation of searchable information constitutes a social good simply because of the available quantity, as "personal information taken out of context often does not foster a more accurate impression of other people."[32]

The result is a situation that Reputation Defender founder Fertik describes as fundamentally *unfair*. This is because the aforementioned factors of permanence, scale, and privileging of salaciousness are combined with what Fertik describes as a kind of interpretive tendency on the part of searchers in which the least charitable information about someone is what is given the most credence. In short, both the information structure *and* the default interpretation of that information have a negative bias. Fertik puts it this way:

> A person tends to get attacked and criticized…usually it's unfairly — it's unfair because it's not true, or it's unfair because it's true but definitely not the whole story. So if you went on a date and the only thing the internet thinks about you is that you are terrible at dates because the one person you went on a date with who was negative decided to attack you online, that's not your full dating history but it's what the internet thinks.

The company Cyber Investigation Services offers a similar cautionary tale about the necessity of staying vigilant about the results that get returned in a search for one's name. They write of a "CEO" who lost control of his online reputation through mere obliviousness:

> Because the CEO was not in the habit of spending much time looking at his online presence, this was not uncovered until potential banking partners discovered it while performing due diligence. Even though the remarks themselves seemed to be so far from reality that the person who wrote them was suspected to be

of unsound mind, the sheer existence of these two blogs were considered unacceptable in the button-down financial world and the deal was scrapped.

Even more disquieting than Fertik's dating example, the implication of this comment seems to be that the veracity of the information is essentially an afterthought; it is the mere taint of association that damages the subject's reputation. Attorney Kenton Hutcherson echoed these characterizations in an interview, and his framing of the situation is particularly interesting in that it implies that there is a kind of rationality to the negative bias in searching:

> on the Internet, there could be 100 good things that about you, but one bad thing is enough to destroy your reputation because people are naturally drawn toward negative information in a fight or flight [sense]; they want to know if there's a danger.

Elsewhere, Fertik has described how the notorious

> 2012 McDonald's spitting incident [in which an employee at a South Carolina McDonalds was charged with food tampering for allegedly spitting in customers' drinks] provides a concrete illustration of this unforgiving dynamic. "Though criminal charges were dropped because the allegations were never proved (and in fact are now suspected to be fake).

Fertik writes, "a Google search for the employee's name years later still brings up articles related to the incident."[33] One would think that the mere presence of something like this might not matter much if evaluated within the overall context of a person's life, but the implication is that it instead becomes the most – or even the only – salient piece of information within the normative parameters of digital-age information-seeking.

Parallel concerns arise with speech about commercial entities. Content marketing expert Christopher Ratcliffe characterizes a similar dynamic as Fertik described above with reference to brands rather than individuals: "[s]ometimes trash-talk is unfair, sometimes it's entirely justified. Unfortunately we don't have a lie detector built into our brains so whenever we read anything negative about a brand we have no reason not to believe it."[34] Some of this "trash talk" might be actionable commercial disparagement, of course, and the attorneys at Esquire Solutions suggest that the ease of sharing opinions and complaints in the digital age does not mean that businesses about whom false statements are made have no recourse: "[I]n a world in which social media gives customers and companies the opportunity to say anything about one another instantly," they argue, "there is a heightened danger of violating the commercial disparagement tort."[35] Nonetheless, this point is predicated on the notion that there is overall a larger volume of speech – much of which is not really subject to any kind of editorial oversight – that is circulating about commercial entities as well as individuals.

A loose consensus has also developed around a corollary result for people who operate a business or sell a product: that the major platforms play such an outsized role in the construction of digital reputations that seemingly minor blemishes can have an outsized effect. News and surveys over the last several years have documented how Amazon sellers routinely beg customers to change negative reviews and offer compensatory incentives to do so. A survey by Seller Labs found that a majority of sellers (which, according to the study's methodology, can be seen as representative of the overall population of sellers) thought that it is "OK to ask buyers to change their product reviews."[36]

While much of the news coverage of the practice has emphasized the irritation that consumers express at this practice, the sentiment from sellers is the result of a common assumption that "a bad review is a fatal blow to us," as one put it in an email to the Wall Street Journal.[37] Likewise, a recent *Wired* article captured the way that this kind of conventional wisdom extends to perceptions about the impact of Google search results on reputation: "[a]s any business that has been downranked by Google's algorithm can tell you, being buried below the first page of results is nearly as bad as being banned."[38] These formulations of the indelible and disproportionate impact of both dubious reputational information as well as lack of visibility online echo one another in their implicit contention that the overwhelming scale and decontextualized nature of the information we encounter online has created a kind of epistemological condition in which information seekers privilege the least flattering interpretation possible when constructing perceptions of those about whom they are seeking information.

Surveys and social scientific studies on the habits of searchers unfortunately suggest several trends that would seem to exacerbate this epistemological tendency. First, web searching is influenced by the cognitive phenomenon that behavioral scientists call "bounded rationality." The fundamental premise of this perspective is that "humans do not always use their cognitive abilities extensively before they make a decision or execute an action...[and] do not consider all possible outcomes before deciding, due to lack of time as well as cognitive constraints."[39] By doing so, however, we are not necessarily behaving irrationally. Rather, "it is reasonable to use simple and faster strategies for decision-making…[as they] take less cognitive effort and, in most cases, are sufficiently efficient."[40] Such an approach is dubbed "satisficing," or the acceptance of an outcome that might theoretically be less than optimal but will suffice for the decision-maker's given objectives.[41]

These concepts have been reflected in research on the habits of search engine users. As an early study by UK researchers on the information literacy of "Google generation" (born 1993 or later), "internet research shows that the speed of young people's web searching means that little time is spent in evaluating information, either for relevance, accuracy or authority."[42] These searchers tend to "assum[e] that search engines "understand" their queries[,] spen[d] little time reading or digesting information and they have difficulty making relevance judgements about the pages they retrieve."[43] Legal scholar James Grimmelman has characterized the overall situation this way:

> Studies have found that users trust search engines, but also that they have woefully poor understandings of how search engines work. The combination is dangerous, because it causes overreliance on search results. Instead of independently evaluating websites for themselves, users invest them with the search engine's authority.[44]

And searchers are apparently only applying this already suboptimal approach to a small subset of results to begin with, as a study by the SEO website Backlink in 2020 revealed that "[o]nly 9% of Google searchers make it to the bottom of the first page of the search results page."[45]

Even if searchers with sub-optimal information literacy are prone to this kind of "satisficing" and bounded rationality, one might still wonder if it is in fact particularly common for individuals to base judgments of people – or even of products and companies – on internet search results to begin with. Yet there is some industry and social science research that indicates the prevalence of such an orientation, and it is taken as axiomatic by reputation management professionals. A non-profit organization devoted to "digital wellbeing" called the Cybersmile Foundation, for instance, asserts that "[m]anaging our reputations on the internet has never been more important," because "the practice of 'checking people out' for potential jobs, relationships and even memberships are now primarily done on the internet by searching popular social media platforms and search engines.["]46 Michael Fertik echoes this sentiment, writing that "[e]ven if you don't use Google to search for gossip, your friends, family, neighbors, and co-workers do." We must therefore take such tendencies seriously, as "[t]he Internet has revealed deeply personal secrets, changed lives, and destroyed families," and these "lies, rumors, and more can affect everyone from PTA moms to soccer dads."[47] This message has evidently been internalized to enough of a degree that one interviewee in a 2014 *New York* magazine article about the practice referred to refraining from the compulsion to Google a potential partner as "the new abstinence."[48] Justine Sacco, a public relations professional who became infamous after a flippant tweet of hers went viral, also echoed the notion that such behavior is commonplace. As she told the journalist Ronson in the aftermath of the incident, "it's not like I can date, because we Google everyone we might date."[49]

Finally, there is in fact some empirical research to suggest that these are common practices as well. A company that provides background screening services called JPD, for instance, conducted a survey about information-seeking habits regarding potential dating partners in 2018 and found that 89% of respondents had done at least some online research about prospective dates in the past (of which 61% said they always or usually did), and 40% said they had even backed out on a date based on what they found.[50] Further, the perception that such behavior is commonplace seems to be reflected in the survey's findings as well, as 63% of respondents said that they would not be embarrassed if it were discovered that they had done such research.[51]

Reputation management professionals often emphasize the degree to which even prospective employers and other potential collaborators search for publicly available information about people online. While the descriptions can sometimes sound both alarmist and vague, they illustrate the general consensus view on the subject. ReputationMaxx CEO Walter Halicki puts it bluntly: [a]lmost anyone who is hiring an employee will check to see what that person looks like online."[52] In another press release, Halicki is more specific about the scrutiny that businesses receive, stating that "90% of consumers look up information online, and 99% of those researchers never look past the first page."[53] Individuals, likewise, must be aware that "[w]e live in an age where someone's page one on Google is their new business card," according to marketing professional Tommy Wyher.[54] Labor market circumstances make it especially imperative that this "business card" be proactively maintained. "Unemployment is at astonishing highs and it's tough to find a job right now," writes one reputation guru named

Andy Beal, and therefore, it is more important than ever to be vigilant and acknowledge the degree to which "Online Reputation Management [sic] is important to your personal brand." This is because "not only are they looking, but 78% of recruiters research a candidate online and 35% actually reject a candidate based on this."

While some such claims are unsourced, the company Internet Reputation bases its warnings[55] on a 2018 survey by the website Career-Builder (conducted by The Harris Poll, a reputable polling outfit), which found that "[s]eventy percent of employers use social networking sites to research job candidates, while seven percent plan to start, [and] of those that do social research, 57 percent have found content that caused them not to hire candidates."[56] An especially revelatory result from the poll concerned the ways in which respondents framed the importance of a personal web presence to begin with. While the headlines from reputation companies usually highlight the dangers of prospective employers finding unflattering content (the categorical characterization of which will also be addressed in more detail in the following chapters), the hiring manager respondents also emphasized that *not* finding anything about a candidate also sets off alarm bells. "Nearly half of employers (47 percent) say that if they can't find a job candidate online, they are less likely to call that person in for an interview," according to the survey, and this response is broken down into two different rationales: "28 percent say that is because they like to gather more information before calling in a candidate for an interview; 20 percent say they expect candidates to have an online presence."[57] In other words, one may be equally penalized for simply *not* cultivating any kind of digital presence.

Such a notion of compulsory participation in digital identity branding helps to characterize how overall, these changes to the information environment that have altered our common "person to public interface" are ultimately taking place within the context of what scholars sometimes call "neoliberal" society. The characterizations of the problem offered by hiring and reputation professionals above are suffused with the values of neoliberalism, as are their strategic recommendations which will be taken up in more detail subsequently. The term neoliberalism is used here to refer to the overarching ideology ascendant toward the end of the twentieth century that combines an emphasis on the economic and political virtues of privatization, free market economics, and a reduced welfare state with a cultural valorization of attitudes like entrepreneurialism and self-help. As used in this book, the term is therefore mainly intended to signify the overlapping cultural and economic frameworks that historian Lisa Duggan describes in her book *The Twilight of Equality*. As she writes, "privatization and personal responsibility" are the terms that "define the central intersections between the *culture* of neoliberalism and its economic vision."[58] This combined cultural and economic sensibility undergirds popular sentiments today regarding the importance and management of reputation as well as (perhaps more implicitly) the receding role of the state in helping to guarantee a life of opportunity and dignity for all citizens.

The conception of identity construction and the corresponding imperative of reputational vigilance on display in the perspectives voiced in this chapter exemplify an additional dimension of the ways in which Marwick has argued that social media reinforces neoliberal subjectivities. The notion of the "self-as-brand" observed by scholars like Vaidhyanathan and Gershon and reinforced by the industry commentators quoted above is indicative of the general logic of "web 2.0" technologies (which includes social media platforms) according to Marwick. In turn, this represents the kind of "infiltration of market logic into everyday social relations" that is characteristic of neoliberal ideology.[59] The ultimate consequence of this is that web 2.0 technologies thus "teac[h] their users to be good corporate citizens in the postindustrial, post-union world by harnessing marketing techniques to boost attention and visibility...they encourage people to regulate their behavior along business ideals."[60]

Formulated this way, therefore, it is unsurprising that some would reframe the situation regarding the unique reputational perils of the digital environment as one rich in opportunity as well. As in Marwick's formulation of the affordances of "self-branding" in the neoliberal tech culture, these commentators implore us to try to make the machinery of online reputation work in our favor. "Rather than fighting it," writes Michael Fertik, "your best option is to curate the kind of digital permanent record that will put you on the right side of this reputation divide."[61] To illustrate the fruits of doing so, Fertik describes how one might unlock more desirable romantic opportunities:

> If you're single and have a positive reputation for romance (and maybe income, intelligence, and other positive qualities), the best dates will come to you without your having to spend hours on dating sites, deal with the "meat market" bar scene, or spend hours cruising phone dating apps.[62]

Elsewhere, he extrapolates this formulation of reputational opportunity to include things like getting better loans, having one's resume picked by automated filtering systems, and selling one's products or services. In short, the contention is that "with the right reputation, the world is your oyster."[63]

In more specific contrast with media scholars like Vaidhyanathan who have written critically about the erosion of reputational control in the digital age, proponents of this kind of "reputational imperative" cast reputation as something newly quantifiable and controllable. The CEO of Klout, a now-defunct company that developed metrics to rate the social influence of social media users, has described reputation-building tactics in terms of a kind of authenticity formula: "You can control your reputation. The top ways to build your online reputation are to make sure your profile reflects who you are and is up-to-date, to be authentic in how you portray yourself, and to be consistent."[64] The company BrandYourself, likewise, frames its service in terms of re-establishing reputational control. "We should all have control over what's out there," states the company's introductory page, and because "you don't want random surprises from social platforms," they "create tools and services that put people back in control of their online reputation."[65] Yet somewhat confusingly, advice to be "authentic" and "control what's out there" is interspersed with other perspectives counseling a more self-inhibiting approach. As one blog asserts, for instance, "[e]mployers would prefer to see photos of involvement with local charities or pictures with family, indications that they are well-rounded, responsible members of society."[66]

While the spirit of empowerment that these perspectives display is thus significant, clearly the situation cannot be resolved simply by encouraging people to be "authentic" and at the same time reductively generic in their self-presentation online. We must therefore consider adaptive endeavors in two broad areas that will take up the remaining empirical focus of the book. First, the reputational vulnerabilities detailed in these critical and industry perspectives on the overall digital information environment prompt questions about whether governments have on some level abdicated their responsibilities to protect citizens from undue harm in their approaches to regulating the internet. The next chapter therefore concerns some of the key legal reforms that have been proposed and enacted in an attempt to rebalance the scale of reputation protection, as well as some criticisms and barriers to their effectiveness.

Further, if we recall from Chapter 1 that legal tools for controlling the circulation of information and vindicating one's reputation also present risks to freedom of expression, and that the kinds of "self-help" approaches to reputation protection sometimes counseled in

the legal context were actually seen as a boon because of their social and practical advantages, we must take the possibility of private
action in mitigating reputational threats seriously rather than simply
dismissing it as another layer of the neoliberal ruse represented by
social media. Correspondingly, then, we will look beyond platitudes
to the complementary reputation management practices that seek to
accomplish via private ordering a version of reputation defense that is
both similar to and distinct from that traditionally offered by law in
the United States.

Notes

1 Siva Vaidhyanathan, *The Googlization of Everything (And Why We Should
   Worry)*. Berkeley: University of California Press (2011), 95.
2 Quoted in David Waller and Rpuert Younger, *The Reputation Game*. London: Oneworld Publicatinos (2017) xv.
3 Vaidhyanathan, *Googlization*, 95.
4 Alice Marwick and danah boyd, "I Tweet Honestly, I Tweet Passionately:
   Twitter Users, Context Collapse, and the Imagined Audience." *New Media
   & Society* 13.1 (2011), 114–33.
5 As Fertik states in an interview with WSI, "Key people at a business are
   inextricably linked in their reputation to that business." WSI, "WSI Digital Insider Series EP 02: Online Reputation Management with Michael
   Fertik" (2015). https://www.youtube.com/watch?v=E-MORGr8Fwk.
6 Alice Marwick and danah boyd, "I tweet honestly, I tweet passionately," 279.
7 Vaidjyanathan, *Googlization*, 72.
8 Ilana Gershon, *Down and Out in the New Economy*. Chicago, IL: University of Chicago Press (2017), 157–58.
9 Gershon, *Down and Out*, 151.
10 Gershon, *Down and Out*, 152.
11 Kristi Piehl, "Determine Your Personal SEO Score." *LinkedIn Blog*,
   July 16, 2020. https://www.linkedin.com/pulse/determine-your-personal-
   seo-score-kristi-piehl.
12 Susan Joyce, "Case Study: How Name Confusion Can Make Your
   Job Search More Difficult." *Job-Hunt*, n.d. https://www.job-hunt.org/
   defensive-googling-mistaken-online-identity/.
13 Joyce, "Defensive Googling."
14 http://austin.craigslist.org/cps/5324514550.html (screen capture saved).
15 Daniel J. Solove, "Speech, Privacy, and Reputation on the Internet." In
   Martha Nussbaum and Saul Levmore (Eds.), *The Offensive Internet*. Cambridge, MA: Harvard University Press (2010), 16.
16 Solove, "Speech, Privacy, and Reputation on the Internet," 17.
17 Solove, "Speech, Privacy, and Reputation on the Internet," 16.
18 Cleverism, "Reputation.com | Interview with its Founder & Execu-
   tive Chairman – Michael Fertik" (2016). https://www.youtube.com/
   watch?v=0eMeOE0sXrc.
19 Solove, "Speech, Privacy, and Reputation on the Internet," 16.
20 Solove, "Speech, Privacy, and Reputation on the Internet on the Internet," 16.

21 Jason Newman, "Jon Ronson: Why We Should Forgive Infamous Tweeter Justine Sacco." *Rolling Stone* (2015, March 31). http://www.rollingstone.com/culture/features/jon-ronson-why-we-should-forgive-infamous-tweeter-justine-sacco-20150331.

22 Kate Eichhorn, *The End of Forgetting*. Cambridge, MA: Harvard University Press (2019), 23.

23 Lauren Goode, "I Called Off My Wedding. The Internet Will Never Forget." *Wired*, April 6, 2021. https://www.wired.com/story/weddings-social-media-apps-photos-memories-miscarriage-problem/.

24 Vaidhanathan, *Googlization*, 72.

25 Vaidhanathan, *Googlization*, 72.

26 "Kale Sligh Gives Tips For Personal Web Reputation Management." *MENAFN*, February 2020. https://bit.ly/3CZ7sCg.

27 Newman, "Why We Should Forgive Justine Sacco."

28 Nina Schick, *Deep Fakes: The Coming Infopocalypse*. New York: Twelve Books (2020), 9.

29 Schick, *Deep Fakes*, 7–9.

30 Deeptrace Labs, "The State of Deepfakes: Landscape, Threats, and Impact" (2019), 6. https://regmedia.co.uk/2019/10/08/deepfake_report.pdf.

31 Brian Leiter, "Cyber Cesspools." In Martha Nussbaum and Saul Levmore (Eds.), *The Offensive Internet*. Chicago, IL: University of Chicago Press (2010), 162.

32 Solove, "Speech, Privacy, and Reputation on the Internet," 13.

33 Michael Fertik, *The Reputation Economy: How to Optimize Your Digital Footprint in a World Where Your Reputation Is Your Most Valuable Asset*. New York: Crown Business (2015), 37.

34 https://econsultancy.com/what-is-online-reputation-management-and-should-you-use-it/.

35 https://www.esquiresolutions.com/the-emerging-prevalence-of-commercial-disparagement/.

36 Seller Labs, "Half of Amazon Sellers Believe It Is OK to Ask Buyers to Change a Product Review," November 20, 2018. https://www.sellerlabs.com/blog/half-of-amazon-sellers-ask-buyers-to-change-product-reviews/.

37 Isobel Asher Hamilton, "Amazon Sellers Are Begging People to Delete Negative Reviews and Offering to Double Refunds if They Do, a Report Says." *Business Insider*, August 9, 2021. https://www.businessinsider.com/amazon-refund-sellers-delete-negative-reviews-wsj-2021-8.

38 https://www.wired.com/story/lets-keep-vaccine-misinformation-problem-in-perspective/.

39 Werner Wirth, Tabea Böcking, Veronika Karnowski, and Thilo Von Pape, "Heuristic and Systematic Use of Search Engines." *Journal of Computer-Mediated Communication* 12.3 (2007), 778–800, 779.

40 Wirth et al., *Journal of Computer-Mediated Communication*, 779.

41 Wirth et al., *Journal of Computer-Mediated Communication*, 779.

42 Ian Rowlands, David Nicholas, and Peter Williams, "The Google Generation: The Information Behaviour of the Researcher of the Future." *Aslib Proceedings* 60.4 (2008), 290–310, 295.

43 Rowlands et al., *Aslib Proceedings*, 297.

44 James Grimmelman, "Speech Engines," *Minnesota Law Review* 98 (2014), 909, 868.

45 Brian Dean, "How People Use Google Search." *Backlinko*, August 20, 2020. https://backlinko.com/google-user-behavior.

46 The Cybersmile Foundation, "Reputation Management." n.d. https:// www.cybersmile.org/reputation-management.
47 From wild west 2.0, http://wildwest2.com/.
48 Maureen O'Connor, "The New Abstinence: Not Googling Your Date." *The Cut*, June 22, 2014. https://www.thecut.com/2014/06/new-abstinence-not-googling-your-date.html.
49 Jon Ronson, "How One Stupid Tweet Blew Up Justine Sacco's Life." *New York Times*, February 15, 2015.
50 JPD, "Study: How Single Americans Research Each Other Before Dates." https://www.jdp.com/blog/study-online-dating-statistics/.
51 JPD, "How Single Americans Research Each Other."
52 "Online Reputation Management Techniques: DIY Ways Individuals Can Protect Their Online Image from JW Maxx Solutions." *PR Newswire*, May 22, 2014. https://advance.lexis.com/api/document?collection=news&id=urn:contentItem:5C89-FR91-JB4P-V2RB-00000-00 &context=1516831.
53 "Reputation Management Agency JW Maxx Solutions Offers Effective Methods for Removing Internet Defamation." *PR Newswire*, March 19, 2013. https://advance.lexis.com/api/document?collection=news&id=urn:content Item:580V-0171-JB4P-V2NB-00000-00&context=1516831.
54 Tommy Wyher, "Online Reputation Management Maxims: Protecting Your Brand Online." *Business2Community*, May 28, 2018. https://advance. lexis.com/api/document?collection=news&id=urn:contentItem:5SF1-D55 1-F03R-N24M-00000-00&context=1516831.
55 Internet Reputation, "Reputation Score: What Is It and Why Does It Matter?" July 6, 2021. https://www.internetreputation.com/reputation-score/.
56 Career Builder, "More Than Half of Employers Have Found Content on Social Media That Caused Them NOT to Hire a Candidate, According to Recent CareerBuilder Survey." August 9, 2018. https://press.careerbuilder. com/2018-08-09-More-Than-Half-of-Employers-Have-Found-Content-on-Social-Media-That-Caused-Them-NOT-to-Hire-a-Candidate-According-to-Recent-CareerBuilder-Survey.
57 Career Builder, "More Than Half."
58 Lisa Duggan, *The Twilight of Equality*. Boston, MA: Beacon Press (2003), 12.
59 Alice Marwick, *Status Update: Celebrity, Publicity, and Branding in the Social Media Age*. New Haven, CT: Yale University Press (2013), 5.
60 Marwick, *Status Update*, 12.
61 Fertik, *Reputation Economy*, 36–37.
62 Fertik, *Reputation Economy*, 8.
63 Fertik, *Reputation Economy*, 15.
64 Michael Simmons, "How to Bulletproof Your Reputation." *Forbes*, August 8, 2014. http://www.forbes.com/sites/michaelsimmons/2014/08/11/ how-to-bulletproof-your-reputation-in-the-digital-age/#59a46e633b5b.
65 Sandy Abrams, "Have You Taken Control of Your Online Reputation?" *Huffington Post*, March 31, 2015. http://www.huffingtonpost.com/sandy-abrams/why-you-need-to-take-cont_1_b_6941316.html.
66 Emily Russo, "How Employers Use Social Media to Hire Employees." April 11, 2013. http://causechatter.com/2013/04/11/how-employers-use-social-media-to-hire-employees/.

3 Remedies
Legal Reform

Given these changes in the information landscape and perceptions of its imperatives, how has the law correspondingly adapted to protect citizens from what are perceived to be new vectors of reputational harm? The perception among many commentators and segments of the general public is that US law does not go far enough to protect against the unique threats to reputation in the digital age. In particular, the precise judicial and policy decisions that arguably enabled the interactive web to grow as robustly and quickly as it has are now seen by many as an impediment to justice for victims of harmful speech. This chapter outlines the relatively limited adaptations in US law and contrasts them with the central European legal reform to address reputational precariousness online, the law colloquially known as the "Right to Be Forgotten." While it concludes that a reform effort on par with the RTBF would be inconsistent with core tenets of American tort and constitutional law, exploring how the RTBF both offers additional redress as well as prompts unique concerns around freedom of expression sets the parameters for our subsequent analysis of how reputation management represents a substitute via private ordering.

American Law and Digital Reputation

To be sure, some legal reforms in the United States have succeeded in addressing novel reputational threats – specifically regarding the new kinds of speech and information online that are technically true but seen as unreasonably harmful nonetheless because of their private nature or widespread visibility. What criminologist Ryan Watstein labels the "criminal record revolution," for instance, has provided employers with greater means of discovering conduct in a prospective employee's past that could portend future problems.[1] In turn, employers have incurred greater risk of liability for negligent hiring.[2] In response,

DOI: 10.4324/9781003287384-4

several states have enacted statutes granting liability from negligent hiring for employers that hire ex-offenders. Ohio, for instance, passed legislation to shield employers from liability for hiring employees who had obtained "certificates of qualification for employment" from a court of common pleas, and for the retention of employees absent actual knowledge of further criminal activity.[3]

Likewise, search results that include incendiary but unambiguously non-fabricated information may stigmatize a person even if they are fundamentally a victim of someone else's wrongdoing. In this vein, nonconsensual pornography (NCP), or "revenge porn," defined as the "re-distribution or dissemination of intimate images without the consent of the subject and without a legitimate purpose,"[4] has also inspired a flurry of legal experimentation in recent years. Because "NCP victims increasingly suffer serious professional damages, which are exacerbated as employers increasingly utilize internet resources to investigate the background of current and prospective employees," states have rushed to criminalize NCP with the hope of deterring it.[5] California passed the first statute expressly addressing NCP in 2013, and 45 other states and the District of Columbia and Guam have since passed some form of anti-NCP legislation.[6] The popularization of the colloquial moniker "revenge pornography" reflects how initial perspectives on the issue assumed that the material was used primarily for harassment or other vengeful purpose, but more recent research has found that such motivations only make up roughly 12% of instances in which NPC was shared.[7] As a result, while some of the variation in the statutes is on account of uncertainty around what courts will deem constitutional, the most successful statutes "focus on the issue of the victim's lack of consent for the defendant to distribute the intimate image and that have fewer additional essential elements."[8]

Yet the overarching approach taken by Congress and the Supreme Court to regulate the internet at its inception has put much more emphasis on limiting the liability of intermediaries for third-party speech. In the seminal *Reno v. ACLU* (1997) case, the Court struck down provisions requiring website operators and users of interactive forums to ensure that they did not "initiat[e] any comment, request, suggestion, proposal, image, or other communication which is obscene or indecent, knowing that the recipient of the communication is under 18 years of age" under threat of criminal sanction.[9] Justice Stevens' opinion took issue with the burdens this kind of requirement would impose on both websites and users (outlined in the "safe harbor" provisions of that same section of the statute): they could use credit card verification as a proxy for age, for instance, but this would impose unreasonable costs on websites for which commercial transactions were otherwise irrelevant and would effectively ban web users who did not own credit cards.

In essence, the Court reasoned that encouraging a form of self-help on the part of the user would be a much less restrictive manner of ensuring that minors did not access adult materials if this was indeed the outcome desired. Parents could monitor their children's internet use, or they could install commercially available filtering software themselves rather than burdening all intermediaries. The *Reno* case therefore saw the Court embracing a vision for speech on the internet in which users and the proprietors of web services would be largely left to manage the flow of available content for themselves.

Another part of the CDA did not receive any constitutional challenge but would prove arguably more consequential for the regulation of speech online.[10] Section 230 decreed that providers of what was categorized as "interactive computer services" (which encompasses both the providers of internet service like Comcast but also web applications like search engines or a user-generated content platform like YouTube) be granted limited liability protections for speech by third parties. Section 230 stipulates that "[n]o provider or user of an interactive computer service shall be treated as the publisher or speaker of any information provided by another information content provider."[11] In other words, hosts of third-party speech are by default merely conduits who provide a platform for speech. It does not, of course, mean that they are not speakers themselves in any capacity or that they are free of other statutorily imposed liabilities (like distribution of copyrighted content). This default only holds as long as the editorial or design parameters of the platform do not play such an integral role in actively "developing" the content submitted by third parties that they have effectively published it.[12]

Section 230 was actually conceived as a means of encouraging web intermediaries to take an active role in monitoring or filtering content by freeing them from liability as speakers if they chose to do so. Subsection (c)(2) exempts providers or users from civil liability for any attempt to block or filter content found to be objectionable regardless of whether it may be well within the ordinary ambit of First Amendment protection.[13] The idea, therefore, was that the safe harbor provision would obviate the need for more intrusive government regulation of speech on the internet by giving content providers incentives to police their own platforms – or to be "good samaritans," as the section's unofficial title put it.

According to some critics, the interpretation of Section 230 in the courts has actually fomented the opposite approach. The seminal interpretation of the scope of Section 230 came in a 1996 Fourth Circuit case called *Zeran v. America Online.* This interpretation foreclosed not only the treatment of interactive computer services as the publishers of third-party statements (which is plainly indicated in the text) but as *distributors* as well. Distributors can generally be held liable for content that they help to circulate if they know or have reason to know that it is tortious or illegal in some way. In Zeran's case, this meant that America Online[14] could not be held liable for an anonymous user's flagrant impersonation of Zeran on AOL chat rooms. This impersonation was allegedly harming Zeran, as it included Zeran's home address and phone number and instructed readers to "call Ken" if they were interested in inflammatory shirts mocking the 1995 Oklahoma City bombing. The court reached this conclusion even though AOL had failed to remove the posts once notified that the posts were false and that Zeran was receiving a high volume of threatening phone calls.[15]

The prevalence of anonymity on the internet makes this decision particularly problematic for some. As the *Zeran* court saw it, the proper method of redress in this kind of situation was to find the speaker and either pursue self-help measures (such as convincing him or her to remove the posts voluntarily) or to sue him or her for defamation in the absence of cooperation. The problem, obviously, is that many potential defendants are difficult to find because so many venues for this kind of speech on the internet afford mostly anonymous activity. The *Zeran* interpretation of Section 230 thus complicates what many see as the imperative to engage in self-help regarding perceived injuries resulting from online speech. The legal hurdles that one faces in trying to discover the identity of an anonymous poster from an ISP are formidable, as one would have to file multiple subpoenas to get the information from ISPs and might have a difficult time identifying the proper jurisdiction for suing anonymous "John Does." Law professor William Frievogel thus wonders whether such a regime effectively "fosters indecency" and distorts the original impetus for Section 230 in the first place, which was to encourage website operators and ISPs to be *proactive* in addressing harm that might be occurring over their platforms. Instead, it appears that websites more often than not use Section 230 as an excuse to abdicate any responsibility for involvement in monitoring and regulating the content that they in some way facilitate.

Referring to the AutoAdmit saga discussed earlier, Frievogel's article describes what was required for one of the targets to actually pursue a legal case:

> Section 230 barred a successful suit against AutoAdmit.com, but the women had a strong enough case to persuade a court to strip

away the anonymous mask of the defamers…[t]hey eventually identified eight of the defamers and obtained settlements from them.[16]

The fact that this victim of the AutoAdmit posters was able to pursue legal action against the perpetrators without wielding some kind of takedown mandate against the platform is auspicious for those who see lifting Section 230s safe harbor as a threat to free speech. At the same time, it is difficult to ignore the extraordinary tenacity required to pursue this kind of legal action. One can reasonably conclude that the legal system is inadequate to redress common newfangled reputational harms that occur online if only the most self-confident, socially assertive, and (probably) resource-rich who can effectively confront offensive or even false speech.

European Law and Digital Reputation: The Right to Be Forgotten

This state of affairs in the United States contrasts markedly with the approach taken in Europe. The Right to Be Forgotten represents a distinct entry in the mosaic of digital-age legal experimentation. What sets it apart from even the limited US reforms described above is that it addresses not simply the consequences or uses of information but its *visibility* in itself. After several years of implementation, the Right to Be Forgotten appears to effectively address some of the unique digital reputational threats outlined in Chapter 2 and the limitations of US law covered in the first part of this chapter. It likewise also illustrates some of the possibilities for overzealous application and abuse that must be taken into account in assessing the impact of both legal reforms and private reputation management practices on the marketplace of ideas.

This section outlines the development of the RTBF through case law, its statutory revisions in the 2018 General Data Protection Regulation (GDPR), and the available public data regarding Google's implementation of its provisions.[17] First, it attempts to map comprehensively the various provisions in the GDPR that offer some mechanisms for balancing the rights to information and expression of internet users with the data privacy rights of data subjects. From this foundation, it then examines how the case of *GC et al v. CNIL* (2019), arguably the most significant ruling on Google's delisting obligations under the newest data protection law, has further framed the scope of the RTBF, and assesses the implications of both the aggregate statistics and delisting request examples in Google's published transparency reports detailing their compliance efforts. Overall, this portrait of the architecture, interpretation, and implementation of the RTBF is intended to highlight the corresponding gaps in the American situation that reputation management practices might fill.

The Origin and Evolution of the Right to Be Forgotten

The RTBF was born from the 2014 decision by the Court of Justice of the European Union (CJEU) in *Google Spain SL, Google Inc v. Agencia Española de Protección de Datos (AEPD), Mario Costeja González.* The decision hinged on a determination of how the requirements set forth in the European Union's 1995 Data Protection Regulation should apply to Costeja's request to the Spanish Data Protection Authority (which will hereafter be referred to as a "DPA") to have Google delist links to a decades-old newspaper article reporting on his bankruptcy proceedings that were still being returned as results for a Google search of his name.

Article 8 of the EU Charter of Fundamental Rights guarantees that [e]veryone has the right to the protection of personal data concerning him or her," and that

> [s]uch data must be processed fairly for specified purposes and on the basis of the consent of the person concerned or some other legitimate basis laid down by law. Everyone has the right of access to data which has been collected concerning him or her, and the right to have it rectified.[18]

The 1995 EU Data Protection Directive represented the seminal framework for guaranteeing the rights in Article 8 with regard to personal data. Among other requirements, it specified the responsibilities and limitations that applied to "data controllers" regarding "the collection and use of personal data," mandated the creation of "an independent national body responsible for the supervision of any activity linked to the processing of personal data" in each member state of the EU (which became the DPAs), and guaranteed a "right to object" for individuals (referred to as "data subjects" in the regulation) via the aforementioned "independent national bodies."[19] The RTBF thus represents an extension of the aims of the Directive – specifically, a newfangled means of ensuring Article 8s "right to have [personal data] rectified."

Under the terms of the Directive, the CJEU concluded that Costeja was entitled to have the links delisted in Google search results for his name. As an important threshold issue, it determined that Google was in fact a "data controller" in the circumstance in question, thus meaning it was subject to the provisions of the directive concerning the processing of personal data. In particular, it noted that Google's search indexing function made it a distinct type of data controller: it reasoned that "web search engines aggregate disparate, previously unconnected information to establish a more or less detailed profile of the data subject" in the form of search results.[20] The newspaper in which the bankruptcy auction announcement was printed was itself not engaging in this type of particularly invasive processing, so the underlying article itself was not in contravention of the rules of the Directive. It was only Google's specific form of search indexing that triggered application of the protections found in Articles 12, 6, and 14 of the Directive. These provisions afford the data subject three central rights: the right to "erasure or blocking of data…because of the incomplete or inaccurate nature of the data"; the right for their "personal data to be kept in a form which permits identification of data subjects for no longer than is necessary for the purposes for which the data were collected"; and the "right to object at any time on compelling legitimate grounds relating to his particular situation to the processing of data relating to him" (though this third provision is subject to exceptions as are determined to be necessary by the particular member states).[21]

While the CJEU acknowledged the need for a "balance to be struck between the data subject's right to privacy and the rights and legitimate interests of internet users in accessing personal data" (which would be mainly predicated on the "'the role played by the data subject in public life'"),[22] the rights of the data subject "override, as a rule, not only the economic interest of the operator of the search engine but also the interest of the general public in having access to that information upon a search relating to the data subject's name."[23] In general, then, the standard that emerged from the Costeja case for what would colloquially be known as the "Right to Be Forgotten" was the following:

> where a person requests the removal of material from a search engine and, following a search on the basis of that person's name, it is found that the results include links to third-party web pages that contain information that is inadequate, irrelevant or excessive to the purposes of the processing by the SEO, the links (and associated information) must be erased.[24]

The General Data Protection Regulation that went into effect in May 2018 replaced the 1995 Directive as the master data protection regulation in the EU. The GDPR re-codified many elements of the earlier

Directive while also expanding several key provisions. Most fundamentally, it expanded the range of categories of "personal data" to things like social networking posts and browsing data that were not contemplated in the 95 Directive.[25] It also creates the new category of "data processor" – essentially, an entity that processes data at the behest of a data controller – to which a more limited set of obligations applies.[26] Finally, the GDPR mandates stiff penalties for breaches of a data subject's rights, including fines of up to 4% of company revenue or 20 million Euros.[27] And alongside the GDPR, national and EU courts have begun to issue rulings interpreting the boundaries of the justifications when Google declines to delist, which has created what Daphne Keller calls "a small but growing body of precedent."[28]

Having reviewed the foundational architecture and impetus of the RTBF and its extension in the GDPR, we can now assess the following: have the GDPR updates perhaps provided more guidance for Google and other data controllers in their responses to requests from data subjects or muddled the waters further? Have the courts helped to clarify major disputes over the boundaries of the law in particular circumstances? And how does the available record of Google's (and other data controllers') decisions suggest that these guidelines are being put into practice by data controllers?

Balancing Data Privacy and Freedom of Expression in the GDPR

Article 17 of the GDPR is the section that spells out the specific provisions of what it now calls the "right to erasure." Its characterizations of the circumstances in which a data subject is entitled to erasure are reminiscent of the "inadequate, irrelevant or excessive to the purposes of the processing" characterization in the Costeja case, but the Article 17 provisions also appear somewhat broader in scope. Paraphrased from the text, a data subject has the right to erasure when: the processing is "no longer necessary in relation to the purposes for which they were collected or otherwise processed," when the subject withdraws consent, when the data is "unlawfully processed," when compliance with another EU or member state law requires erasure, and when data pertaining to minors has been collected pursuant to an offer of "information society services" (which, the UK Information Commissioner's office clarifies, "essentially means most online services").[29]

Article 17(1)(c), furthermore, states that a data subject is entitled to erasure when they object pursuant to another provision, Article 21(1), which itself entitles the data subject to object to processing that has been justified by the controller under its general parameters for lawful processing under Article 6(1). Article 6(1) lays out the blanket justifications for processing itself, including things like the execution of a contract and

> processing [that] is necessary for the purposes of the legitimate interests pursued by the controller or by a third party, except where such interests are overridden by the interests or fundamental rights and freedoms of the data subject which require protection of personal data.[30]

Article 21 itself describes the exceptions to its application in similar terms, saying it applies "unless the controller demonstrates compelling legitimate grounds for the processing which override the interests, rights and freedoms of the data subject or for the establishment, exercise or defence of legal claims."[31] In sum, article 17(1)(c) essentially appears to offer a catch-all provision in which the data subject enjoys the right to erasure if they object to the processing – unless the controller can show "compelling legitimate grounds for the processing" that override the data subject's rights (which, presumably, means the general formulation of privacy rights in the European Charter of Fundamental Rights). In other words, Article 17 of the GDPR appears to give fairly broad latitude to subsequent interpreters to decide what when the right to erasure in fact applies.

The RTE for data subjects articulated in Article 17(1)–(2) is subject to two other textual exceptions that aim to balance the rights of data subjects with freedom of expression and access to information. First, there is a third section of Article 17 itself which declares that the preceding sections do not apply when the processing has been undertaken "for exercising the right of freedom of expression and information."[32] Then, the RTE provisions are also subject to a textually distinct (but obviously substantively overlapping) set of limitations related to freedom of expression that are spelled out in Article 85 of the GDPR. EU law has traditionally balanced data privacy and freedom of expression: the Charter of Fundamental Rights, for instance, also contains Articles guaranteeing "freedom of thought, conscience, and religion," as well as "freedom of expression and information."[33] GDPR Article 85 specifically directs EU member states to create legal exemptions for the data protection provisions of the GDPR when the data processing is "carried out for journalistic purposes or the purpose of academic artistic or literary expression."[34]

While most of the member states appear to have amended their Data Protections Regulations to include such exemptions, they vary in their wording and scope. Germany's Regulation, for instance, appears to offer a relatively limited exemption "where the erasure is...impossible, or only possible with disproportionately high effort and the data subject has a minor interest for erasure." Ireland, on the other hand, applies the exemption in Section 43(1) of its law to "the processing of personal data for the purpose of exercising the right to freedom of expression and information, *including* [italics added] processing for journalistic purposes or for the purposes of academic, artistic or literary expression," thus suggesting that the categories named in GDPR Article 85 are merely a starting point. At the other end of the spectrum, the Spanish DPA has been slow to amend its act to reflect the Article 85 requirements, merely referencing the text of the GDPR itself. Overall, though, a majority of member states appear to have explicitly included the section of the GDPR containing the Right to Erasure in their list of exemptions for the processing of data for journalistic, academic, artistic, and literary expression.

While the categories named in GDPR Article 85 are indeed important categories of speech to safeguard, Daphne Keller also points out that "valuable online expression often falls outside of those four enumerated categories."[35] For instance, "[a] tweet about a dishonest car mechanic, a Yelp review of a botched medical procedure, or a post criticizing an individual Etsy or Amazon vendor...[or] a personal blog post recounting domestic abuse" might not fall into one of the privileged categories named in the text, but they undoubtedly represent important expression, or what Keller calls the "democratic cacophony that makes the internet so different from prior speech platforms."[36]

Overall, then, the text of the new legislation itself appears to have modestly expanded the categorical protections for data subjects and raised the stakes for noncompliance via fines. At the same time, it also offers a patchwork of possible exceptions through which data controllers can justify their processing on freedom of expression and public interest grounds, but the scope of these exceptions is largely left to the discretion of Data Protection Authorities and Courts to determine on a case-by-case basis.

Clarifying the Obligations of Search Engines: GC et al. v. CNIL

Case law from the Court of Justice of the European Union (CJEU) has offered some clarification as to the territorial applicability of the

GDPR itself[37] and the scope of several of its requirements for data controllers. In the 2019 case *GC and Others v. CNIL*, the CJEU helped to clarify aspects of how the new law applies to search engines as a specific kind of data controller – or as the authors of one case comment put it, the case represents "Google Spain Balancing Through [the] GDPR Lens."[38]

The GC case involves a composite of four delisting requests that were rejected first by Google and then by CNIL, the French DPA. Upon the plaintiffs' appeal to the French Council of State court, the Court asked the CJEU for clarification of a number of questions regarding the delisting responsibilities of search engines. Specifically, the links at issue in the *GC* case all involved what the GDPR (and the 95 Directive before it) calls "special categories of personal data." These include:

> personal data revealing racial or ethnic origin, political opinions, religious or philosophical beliefs, or trade union membership, and the processing of genetic data, biometric data for the purpose of uniquely identifying a natural person, data concerning health or data concerning a natural person's sex life or sexual orientation.[39]

Correspondingly, Article 10 of the GDPR also establishes limitations on the processing of personal data related to criminal offenses, stipulating that "processing shall be carried out only under the control of official authority or when the processing is authorised by Union or Member State law providing for appropriate safeguards for the rights and freedoms of data subjects."[40] This processing is to be prohibited by data controllers unless they can demonstrate that the data subject consented, that the data has been "manifestly made public" by the subject themselves, or if the "processing is necessary for reasons of substantial public interest."[41] In its request, the French Court asked the CJEU to clarify how these prohibitions (and accompanying exceptions) apply to Google (or any search engine) in light of its unique processing role in making data published on other websites visible in a query for a person's name.[42]

First, the CJEU opinion clarified when the obligation is in fact triggered for the search engine processor. The text of the law technically suggests that the obligations of controllers are "triggered once their 'activity is liable to affect significantly the fundamental rights to privacy and to the protection of personal data,'" but taken at face value, this would mean that search engines had an obligation to proactively screen search results.[43] In noting the practical impossibility of doing so, the Court thus clarified that the obligations "will apply to search engines only upon a delisting request by the data subject," thus in effect confirming that the system will work in a "notice-and-takedown" fashion that is reminiscent of other areas of intermediary liability law.[44]

In addressing the more substantive balancing questions, the Court emphasized that it is the search engine itself that plays the critical role in weighing the public interest considerations pursuant to the rights of freedom of expression and access to information with the particular impact that the data is likely to have on the data subject's right to privacy – particularly in cases where significant time has elapsed and its relevance to the subject's current life has perhaps become attenuated.[45] Thus, it declined to issue any precise test for determining when one interest outweighs the other, simply encouraging Google to carry out its responsibility to weigh the interests with a special sensitivity to whether

> the inclusion of that link in the list of results displayed following a search on the basis of the data subject's name is *strictly necessary* [italics added] for protecting the freedom of information of internet users potentially interested in accessing that web page by means of such a search.[46]

While Google is being encouraged to delist when there are other means for an internet user to discover the information in question, if Google *does* determine that the freedom of information interests necessitate preserving the indexing of links in a search for the data subject's name specifically (because, presumably, they are essential to the legitimate public interest in that person), then it seems to have the court's blessing.

Regarding the balancing of considerations in delisting requests related to criminal offenses specifically, the Court was more forthcoming with additional evaluative criteria. In situations where a delisting request is made specifically for links that pertain to an "earlier stage of the proceedings" before a criminal charge was fully adjudicated (which was the basis of plaintiff BH's delisting request), the Court asserted that the search engine should consider the following:

> [W]hether, in the light of all the circumstances of the case, such as, in particular, the nature and seriousness of the offence in question, the progress and the outcome of the proceedings, the time elapsed, the part played by the data subject in public life and his past conduct, the public's interest at the time of the request, the content and form of the publication and the consequences of publication for the data subject, he or she has a right to the information in

question no longer, in the present state of things, being linked with his or her name by a list of results displayed following a search carried out on the basis of that name.

Thus, while the criteria listed are numerous, the direction is again simply for the search engine to engage in its own balancing of the factors to determine whether the data subject deserves to have the information not be prominently associated with them via name search results.

Balancing Data Subjects' Right with the Public Interest: Google's Delisting Decisions

How, then, has Google approached this balancing? While Google does not report European Right to Erasure requests to the Lumen Database for review by researchers, the company does publish transparency reports disclosing aggregate statistics and anonymized explanations of what it frames as simply "examples of requests [they] have received."[47] The aggregate statistics break down requests categorically in terms of requesters, type of content, and type of website.

Perhaps the most striking statistic regarding requesters that the report offers is that roughly 1% of requesters make up 20% (or 1.4 million) of the total requests for delisting, though this statistic is only reported in the current transparency report through January of 2018.[48] When broken down by subcategory of requester, nearly 90% of requests come from requesters classified as "private individuals," with the remaining requests coming from a mix of corporate representatives, public officials, non-political public figures, and parties acting on the behalf of minors (with minors and the other categories combined each accounting for roughly half of these requests). Thus, while it appears that a small subset of requesters is using the RTBF to target large numbers of links and thus potentially impact great swaths of information about a particular data subject, the law is nonetheless overwhelmingly being used to delist links pertaining to private individuals in whom no generalized public interest exists.

The subject matter breakdown of requests and delisted links first indicates that a large percentage of requests concern links for which there is no real substantive balancing to engage in (over 40% since the collection began, and over 46% since the implementation of the GDPR). Requests in one such category – those containing insufficient information to render a decision (such as incomplete URLs in the request) are summarily rejected. The other such category, requests in which the name of the requester is not actually found in the link, are summarily granted (since there is no reason for the page to be showing up in search results for the person's name).[49]

Most of the other subject matter categories display relatively stable rates of delisting since Google began tracking the data in January 2016. Other than the two covered above, links in the category "professional information" (which Google explains as "content [that] contains a requester's work address, contact information, or general information about their business activities")[50] are the most likely to be requested for delisting, and they have been delisted at a rate that has ranged between 15% and 25% over the five-plus years. Requests to delist content in the "political," category, in which "[p]age content contains criticism of a requester's political or government activities or information that is relevant to the individual's public political history, platform, or profile," are almost never granted.[51] This reflects the strong recognition in the GDPR and case law that the default deference to data subjects is mitigated by the subject's role in public life.

The other categories of "crime," "professional wrongdoing," "self-authored," and "personal information" all garner between roughly 6% and 7% of requests, but they are delisted at different rates. Professional misconduct, perhaps surprisingly, is also delisted in the 15–25% range, with crime delisted at an even higher rate of between 40% and almost 70% during the five-year period (with a pronounced trend upward starting at the beginning of 2019 and leveling off slightly at over half in 2021). While these might seem like categories of information in which there would be substantial public interest, the following discussion of the delisting decision examples will explore how this is likely due to the particular kinds of past transgressions that are most commonly requested for delisting.

Several impressions can be gleaned from the anonymized examples of individual requests provided in the transparency report. These are the weight given to the passage of time in delisting decisions, the degree to which the decisions often depend on the data subject's current professional and personal endeavors, the influence that the presence of "sensitive data" seems to exert on the decisions in which it is a factor, the willingness to delist links pertaining to "spent convictions"[52] and other minor criminal offenses (subject to the above criteria as well), and, finally, the perhaps surprising willingness to delist based on the above criteria even for serious crimes.[53]

The passage of time appears to be the most common factor cited in Google's decisions about delisting, and serves as justification for both approval and denial. One request from the Italian DPA, for instance, was rejected due to the lack of time that had passed since "a business consultant [was] involved in an investigation for crimes connected to an organized crime group." On the other hand, the passage of time was cited as the reason to approve delisting for "6 news articles reporting on a private injury claim he brought against the security staff of a night club in 2010," even though the subject was later found to have mislead the court about the incident and the articles simply mentioned his case as part of a larger general exploration of the role of social media in court cases. Ten years was thus determined to be a significant enough passage of time to render the subject deserving of being disassociated from the incident in name search results. And while the articles certainly represent publicly important discussion in themselves, it is important to remember that the delisting only applies to results for the subject's name, meaning, for instance, that a search for "social media in court cases" might well still turn up the links in question.

The passage of time is frequently cited, but it is also usually accompanied by a supporting rationale. This most often involves the lack of (or continued) relevance of the link to the subject's current endeavors. One request from "a former city level active member of a German right-wing party to remove 17 URLs from Google search" was granted, for instance, because "the individual had left the party several years ago." A request to delist URLs pertaining to "the individual's position as the leader of the youth wing of a political party as a minor" was also granted because there was no evidence that the individual was still active in politics. On the other hand, quite a number of the requests even within this relatively small sample (in the grand scheme of the millions of requests Google has received) were rejected because the information contained in the links appeared still relevant to the subject's current position or activities. A request to delist links that "recounted how an individual's former company was accused of not paying its employees and becoming subject to bankruptcy procedures" was denied because the subject was still working in the same area of business; another regarding links to a "report about a multimillion-Euro summary judgment order obtained by a bank against the individual regarding a prior loan" was also denied because the subject was still running the same business; and in an especially fact-intensive example, a "high-ranking executive" requested that 45 URLs delisted that referenced his involvement in the case. While the individual did provide Google with court documents indicating that the case had been "dismissed on technical grounds," Google still did not delist the links because the documents did not actually contain any conclusive indication of his guilt or innocence. Overall, the decision in 23 out of the 96 request examples reviewed hinged centrally on the relevance of the links to the requester's current endeavors (whether professionally or personally).

A final major category of delisting decisions covered in the examples concerns links pertaining to criminal charges, proceedings, and convictions. Though it extends back to before the GDPR, the Transparency Report evinces a clear effort (in accordance with the CJEU's prompt in the GC case) to delist links for a name search that do not reflect the ultimate outcome of a case. In instances where an individual was charged with a crime but never convicted, for example, the mere association of the individual with the charges can create an impression of impropriety for an internet searcher that misrepresents the data subject. One request that Google granted in this vein involved a news reporter who was "accused of rape over 15 years ago, but acquitted... [and] [t]he court proceedings were heavily covered in the media at the time." In a variation on this theme, Google also appears to commonly grant delisting requests if the links pertain to spent convictions or simply very old or minor convictions (implicitly accompanied by the caveat that the data subject does not appear to have had further legal trouble more recently). It granted a request for links that "report about the arrest of the individual in the United States for theft," for example, and even a request from a "high-ranking government official" to delist 124 links because the official had been implicated in a corruption scandal but never convicted.

On the other hand, some of the company's treatment of links pertaining to particularly severe crimes and the apparent weight it gives to the presence of sensitive personal information in crime-related delisting decisions might give some pause. A link that "reporting on [an] individual's escape from a mental hospital where he was undergoing treatment for schizophrenia" was delisted because it (unsurprisingly) contained "sensitive information about his mental health." The fact that the individual had been "found guilty but not criminally responsible for a murder" was not enough to sway the balance against delisting. And though it was done to comply with a court order from a court in the Netherlands, the company also delisted links "that reported on a landlord's conviction for secretly recording female tenants in the shower" because the court had "argued that the URL contained sensitive personal data and the public interest was not substantial enough to justify the indexing of the URL." Perhaps more alarmingly, another request was granted for the delisting of a link that "related to the sentencing of the individual to ten years for the murder of their partner" with the passage of time cited as the rationale.

Finally, several examples appear to show delisting being granted for information related to convictions for sexual crimes: one upon request from the French DPA for four links "regarding the sentencing of the individual for a sexual offence against a child and a female adult," another delisting "a blog post from Google Search that discussed the doctor's conviction for sexually harassing a teenage girl," and another for "[p]age content [that] reported on the arrest and sentencing of the individual for possessing child pornography and attempting to have sex with a child" – though the report does note that the sentence referred to in the post was incorrectly high. While the decisions are again highly context-dependent, one might reasonably object that such cases are so severe that neither passage of time nor incidental inclusion of sensitive information or nominal errors should be grounds for de-linking the information from a search of the individual's name.

The Implications of the RTBF for the United States

Overall, then, while the RTBF generally represents a fundamentally different approach to balancing privacy and reputation with freedom of expression than does American law, the GDPR offers myriad ways in which a data controller (including but not limited to Google) *can* justify its processing on freedom of expression or public interest grounds. The significant judicial precedents to this point have declined to interpret these defenses uncharitably, instead simply emphasizing the need for Google (and implicitly other controllers) to balance the numerous but clearly articulated competing interests judiciously in response to the particulars of each situation. With this latitude, Google appears to have settled on a general approach that privileges the passage of time and the information's relevance to the requester's present endeavors in its delisting decisions – in other words, a means for the information profile of a data subject to effectively "catch up" to the person's current situation. One of the implications for the United States, therefore, is that the European experience with the RTBF thus far suggests that private intermediaries are indeed capable of making large-scale categorical changes to the way they handle novel reputational harms in a reasonably systematic manner.

On the other hand, however, the mere fact that the RTBF does not seem to have posed a grave threat to freedom of expression thus far does not mean that its core components do not carry the potential to undermine the marketplace of ideas. The aggregate data and delisting request examples also still suggest that the company must remain vigilant in defending against overzealous delisting attempts (some of

which have been approved by member state Data Protection Authorities themselves), and critical conversations remain regarding the categorical boundaries of prior transgressions that should be delinked
from an individual's name search results. And given its appearance
of privileging the data subject's right to data protection over other
expression-related rights, the general approach embodied by the RTBF
has been viewed with suspicion by a number of freedom of expression
advocates in the United States. Some have highlighted the potential
threat not just to speakers whose speech is delisted from search results,
but for *readers* who seek information. Kristie Byrum, for instance,
has argued that as conceived in the EU, the RTBF "disrupts the information marketplace by compromising the inventory of information
available online."[54] Samuel Royston elaborates on this position by
contending that compelled delisting is tantamount to censorship:

> Instituting the right to be forgotten risks the suppression of collec-
> tive memory…[a]lthough content that is de-linked from search en-
> gine results remains on the actual website on which it is published,
> such information is all but useless if it is not accessible through a
> search engine.[55]

Other scholars have also expressed concern about the way the law
compels Google, a private entity, to act as an arbiter of many decisions
about the public visibility of speech that will for the most part not see
public adjudication: as Jack Balkin writes, for instance, "the European
Union has deputized Google to create a bureaucracy within Google
that will administer the right to be forgotten in the first instance. The
assumption is that Google will settle most of the claims at this level."[56]
Daphne Keller underscores the potential for abuse if indeed most of
the claims are settled at that level:

> RTBF claims [are] uniquely powerful legal tools—both for legit-
> imate claimants and for abusive ones targeting information the
> public has a right to see. A person asserting a RTBF claim can by-
> pass long-standing laws and substantive legal defenses that would
> have shielded lawful speech against other claims based on reputa-
> tional harms, such as defamation or invasion of privacy.[57]

In perhaps a more pragmatic sense, any attempt to implement a similar
law in the United States would likely not pass constitutional muster
in America. As conceived in the aforementioned legislation and cases
and implemented by Google, an identical RTBF law would be difficult

to reconcile with several tenets of American First Amendment law. Most fundamentally, most of the speech that is targeted in the RTBF falls into the category of true speech. The extensive protection granted to true speech was introduced previously via traditionally narrow scope of the public disclosure of private facts tort, which as readers will recall from the overview of the privacy torts in Chapter 1, is the most analogous US cause of action that deals with the kind of true but embarrassing speech that the RTBF seems most intent on remedying. As law professor Jeffrey Toobin notes, the Supreme Court has "c[o]me close to saying, but never quite said, that publication of the truth was always protected by the First Amendment."[58]

As described previously, the public disclosure tort contains an exception for information deemed to be "newsworthy." As drawn up and implemented so far, the RTBF appears to have essentially reframed the categories of speech that get routinely delisted as no longer newsworthy. In America, however, the law has typically deferred to the press to determine what is newsworthy in public disclosure cases. Law professor Diane Zimmerman has described this as the "leave it to the press model," by which "most judges ... accept the press's judgment about what is and is not newsworthy." Further, unlike the stipulation in the European "Right" that search engines should consider the "relevance" (i.e. age) of data, the passage of time has most consistently been found not to mitigate newsworthiness in American tort law.

What about a right to be forgotten mechanism that exclusively applies to false speech? Readers will also recall from the overview of US defamation law that in instances of personal expression (rather than, say, fraudulent material misrepresentation), the trajectory in American law is to err increasingly on the side of protection. In fact, as law professor Clay Calvert has argued, the 2010 *United States v. Alvarez* case held that "[e]ven deliberate, non-libelous falsehoods can be protected," and thus

> to punish false speech via legal mechanisms other than defamation, and fraud, the government would also need to demonstrate what the Supreme Court has called 'a direct causal link' between the speech in question and the problem or harm it supposedly produces

– an insurmountable obstacle in many cases.[59] And though the RTBF does not involve criminal penalties, UN Special Rapporteur David Kaye has pointed out that it is "[r]egimes that are either non-democratic or tend to resist democratic ideals like a free press" that are the ones which "often criminalize false speech" – implying again that democratic societies require greater tolerance for even some false speech in order to achieve robust public discourse.[60]

In addition to the ways in which the RTBF would exceed the boundaries typically envisioned in US tort law for remedying the effects of true speech and even of defamatory falsehoods, the mechanics of the RTBF also conflict with the fundamental notion that the editorial decisions of media and technology companies qualify as "speech" in their own right. In the context of broadcasting, the D.C. Circuit accepted the FCC's argument in the *Syracuse Peace Council* case that it should discontinue part of the Fairness Doctrine because its enforcement "requires the government to second-guess broadcasters' judgment on such sensitive and subjective matters as the 'controversiality' and 'public importance' of a particular issue."

Perhaps most directly relevant to the RTBF is the growing body of argument in the United States asserting that search engine results deserve similar deference as editorial speech. Eugene Volokh and Donald Falk, for instance, have contended that Google's algorithmically ordered judgments about the relevance of links to particular search queries should benefit from the general recognition that "[t]he First Amendment...fully protects Internet speakers' editorial judgments about the selection and arrangement of content." Labeling them "editorial judgments" is significant, as the Supreme Court declared Florida's "right of reply" law for newspapers unconstitutional in *Miami Herald v. Tornillo* (1974) on the reasoning that "the Florida statute fail[ed] to clear the barriers of the First Amendment because of its intrusion into the function of editors."[61]

Legal scholar James Grimmelman, one of the foremost American authorities on internet law, has offered a framework that is somewhat less deferential to search engines, but still proclaims their results to be "opinions about relevance."[62] Even in Grimmelman's framework, in which search engines are conceived of as "advisers" whose rankings should be evaluated according to a version of the actual malice standard (to determine whether they are making reckless or knowingly false recommendations on the results of any given search), a compelled reordering of search results absent an underlying judicial showing of, say, defamation would not presumably pass muster.[63]

Further, the courts that have weighed in on the matter have tended to adopt something closer to the Volokh and Falk position, which Grimmelman labels the "editor theory." A seminal case testing the legal status of Google search results, *Search King v. Google* (2003), reached the conclusion that "'Google's search results were constitutionally protected opinions,' rendering them 'immune from tort liability.'"[64] A similar characterization of the status of search results as speech has been recognized subsequently by the US District Court for the Southern District of NY in 2014, which determined in *Zhang v. Baidu* that "there is a strong argument to be made that the First Amendment fully immunizes search-engine results from most, if not all, kinds of civil liability and government regulation."[65] This principle was subsequently cited approvingly by the District Court for the Southern District of Mississippi in *Google v. Hood*: "the relevant, developing jurisprudence teaches that Google's publishing of lawful content and editorial judgment as to its search results is constitutionally protected."[66] As the Electronic Frontier Foundation summarized in a recent amicus brief,

> [e]very court that has considered the issue, dating back to at least 2007, has rightfully found that private entities that operate online platforms for speech and that open those platforms for others to speak enjoy a First Amendment right to edit and curate that speech.[67]

Overall, the major provisions of the RTBF thus run counter to some of the central principles of tort law and First Amendment doctrine in the United States regarding true speech, the passage of time in determinations of newsworthiness, the rights of intermediaries themselves, and the general weight assigned to privacy and reputation protection versus freedom of speech and access to information. Yet while the RTBF could not be copied statutorily, it nonetheless provides us with some key parameters for thinking about how reputation management practices can fill in the gaps, acting as an "American RTBF" via private ordering.

Notes

1 In general, empirical social science research has long shown that the comprehensiveness and ease of background checks (which today turn up an expanded range of information, such as charges that were never prosecuted) is correlated with decreased employment prospects. See for instance Ryan Watstein, "Out of Jail and Out of Luck: The Effect of Negligent Hiring Liability and the Criminal Record Revolution on an Ex-Offender's Employment Prospects." *Florida Law Review*. 61 (2009), 583.
2 Watstein, "Out of Jail and Out of Luck."
3 Rod Fliegel, William Simmons, and Inna Shelley, "Ohio Joins Handful of States That Offer Tort Liability Protections for Businesses That Hire and Employ Rehabilitated Ex-Offenders." *Littler*, August 10, 2012. https://www.littler.com/ohio-joins-handful-states-offer-tort-liability-protections-businesses-hire-and-employ-rehabilitated.

4 Jonathan Sales and Jessica Magaldi, "Deconstructing the Statutory Landscape of 'Revenge Porn': An Evaluation of the Elements that Make an Effective Non-consensual Pornography Statute." *American Criminal Law Review* 57 (2020), 1499.   https://www.law.georgetown.edu/american-criminal-law-review/in-print/deconstructing-the-statutory-landscape-of-revenge-porn/.

5 Sales and Magaldi, *American Criminal Law Review*, 1509.

6 Sales and Magaldi, *American Criminal Law Review*, 1500.

7 Sales and Magaldi, *American Criminal Law Review*, 1502.

8 Sales and Magaldi, *American Criminal Law Review*, 1500.

9 From 47 U.S. 223, quoted in *Reno v. ACLU*, 521 U.S.844 (1997).

10 In fact, it was originally conceived as a constitutionally unproblematic alternative to the more stringent speech restrictions in Section 223 and elsewhere:

> Cox-Wyden was envisioned as a more effective alternative to the original provisions because it (1) was likely constitutional and (2) would provide a more direct means – self-regulation – of preventing children from accessing inappropriate material. The goal of protecting children, of course, remained broadly similar to that reflected in Senator Exon's proposal.

David Lukmire, "Can the Courts Tame the Communications Decency Act?" *NYU Annual Survey of American Law* 66 (2010), 379.

11 47 U.S.C. 230(c)(1).

12 This is a general paraphrase of the holding in *Fair Housing Council of Greater San Fernando Valley v. Roomates.com LLC*, 489 F.3d 921 (9th Cir., April 3, 2008). Roomates.com attempts to match prospective roommates using their answers to a detailed questionnaire about housing preferences. The FHC contended that Roommates' questions about race and gender preferences were discriminatory under the terms of the Fair Housing Act, but Roommates asserted immunity under Section 230 from liability as the publisher of the content on the site (whether it was discriminatory within the meaning of the FHA or not). The 9th Circuit ruled that 230 did not apply and remanded to the district court regarding the allegedly discriminatory questions. The *Roommates* decision has thus been described as the first major case spelling out a situation in which a putatively passive forum for facilitating exchanges between users can lose its Section 230 immunity when it effectively participates too much in the "development" of the content (even though the actual text is still submitted by users) to contend that it is merely a conduit. See also *FTC v. Accusearch*, 570 F.3d 1187 (2009), in which the Tenth Circuit applied a similar framework.

13 The text reads:

> No provider or user of an interactive computer service shall be held liable on account of—
>
> **(A)** any action voluntarily taken in good faith to restrict access to or availability of material that the provider or user considers to be obscene, lewd, lascivious, filthy, excessively violent, harassing, or otherwise objectionable, whether or not such material is constitutionally protected; or
>
> **(B)** any action taken to enable or make available to information content providers or others the technical means to restrict access to material described in paragraph (1).

14 America Online in its heyday was unlike most of the internet companies that we encounter today in that it provided both the internet service itself (the transmission of packets of data over the last mile to the customer), as well as many of the actual platforms on which users could interact or seek third party content once they were connected to the internet — e.g. chat rooms and the AOL-administered "channels" for news, sports, weather, and the like. Most of the contemporary internet companies do one or the other but not both.

15 *Zeran v. AOL*, 129 F.3d 327 (cert. denied).

16 William Frievogel, "Does the CDA Foster Indecency?" *Communication Law and Policy* 16.1 (2011), 41.

17 It is important to note that critical questions remain regarding the application of the RTBF to other kinds of platforms and content hosts. Legal scholar Daphne Keller, for instance, has argued that a critical point of clarification is necessary regarding how the provisions of the GDPR and RTBF case law apply to social media platforms. Daphne Keller, "The Right Tools: Europe's Intermediary Liability Laws and the Eu 2016 General Data Protection Regulation." *Berkeley Technology Law Journal* 33 (2018), 344–45, 287.

18 European Charter of Fundamental Rights, Article 8(1)–(2).

19 EurLex, "Protection of Personal Data." https://eur-lex.europa.eu/legal-content/EN/LSU/?uri=celex:31995L0046.

20 Keller, "The Right Tools," 324.

21 David Lindsay, "The 'Right to be Forgotten' by Search Engines under Data Privacy Law: A Legal Analysis of the Costeja Ruling." *Journal of Media Law* 6.2 (2014), 159–79, 168–69.

22 Lindsay, *Journal of Media Law*, 171–72.

23 *Google Spain* para. 100(4). https://curia.europa.eu/juris/document/document.jsf?docid=152065&doclang=EN.

24 Lindsay, *Journal of Media Law*, 174.

25 Ivan Klekovic, "EU GDPR vs. European Data Collection Directive." *EU GDPR Blog*, October 30, 2017. https://advisera.com/eugdpracademy/blog/2017/10/30/eu-gdpr-vs-european-data-protection-directive/.

26 The difference can be illustrated by the following: "a bank (controller) collects the data of its clients when they open an account, but it is another organisation (processor) that stores, digitizes, and catalogs all the information produced on paper by the bank." Carla Bouca, EU GDPR Controller vs. Processor. Carla Bouca, "EU GDPR controller vs. processor – What are the differences?" EU GDPR Knowledge base, n.d. https://advisera.com/eugdpracademy/knowledgebase/eu-gdpr-controller-vs-processor-what-are-the-differences/.

27 Klekovic, "GDPR vs. Directive."

28 Keller, "The Right Tools," 326.

29 GDPR Section 17(1)(a)–(b), (d)–(f); UK ICO, "What Are the Rules about an ISS and Content?" https://ico.org.uk/for-organisations/guide-to-data-protection/guide-to-the-general-data-protection-regulation-gdpr/children-and-the-uk-gdpr/what-are-the-rules-about-an-iss-and-consent/#a3.

30 GDPR Article 6(1)(f).

31 GDPR Article 21(1).

32 GDPR Article (17)(3)(a).
33 EU Charter of Fundamental Rights, Article 10; Article 11.
34 GDPR Article 85(2).
35 Keller, "The Right Tools," 354.
36 Keller, "The Right Tools," 355.
37 *Google v. CNIL* (2019). https://curia.europa.eu/juris/document/document. jsf?docid=218105&doclang=EN.
38 Yuliya Miadzvetskaya and Geert Van Calster, "Google at the Kirchberg Dock. On Delisting Requests, and on the Territorial Reach of the EU's GDPR (C-136/17 GC and Others v CNIL, C-507/17 Google Inc v CNIL)." *European Data Protection Law Review* 6.1 (2020), 143–51, 143.
39 GDPR Article 9(1).
40 GDPR Article 10(1).
41 GDPR Article 9(2).
42 GC et al v. CNIL, par. 31.
43 Miadzvetskaya and Calder, "Google at the Kirchberg Dock," 145–46.
44 Miadvzetskaya and Calder, "Google at the Kirchberg Dock," 145–46. The authors note that the system described in the GC case is similar to the approach laid out in the E-Commerce Directive that governs general inter-mediary liability rules in the EU. This is, incidentally, similar to a sugges-tion made by Keller in her critique of the ambiguities present in the GDPR legislative text (pp. 364–65).
45 This emphasis can be observed in its summary answer to the question of how the provisions apply to Google:

> where the operator of a search engine receives a request for de-referencing relating to a link to a web page on which such sensitive data are published, the operator must, on the basis of all the relevant factors of the particular case and taking into account the seriousness of the interference with the data subject's fundamental rights to privacy and protection of personal data laid down in Articles 7 and 8 of the Charter, ascertain, having regard to the reasons of substantial pub-lic interest referred to in Article 8(4) of Directive 95/46 or Article 9(2) (g) of Regulation 2016/679 and in compliance with the conditions laid down in those provisions, whether the inclusion of that link in the list of results displayed following a search on the basis of the data subject's name is strictly necessary for protecting the freedom of information of internet users potentially interested in accessing that web page by means of such a search, protected by Article 11 of the Charter.
> GC et al., par. 68

46 GC et al., par. 69.
47 Requests to delist content under European privacy law. https://transparen-cyreport.google.com/eu-privacy/overview.
48 Requests to delist content under European privacy law, "Categories of Requesters."
49 "Categories of Content Requested for Delisting"; "Requested URL Delis-ting Rate by Category."
50 European Privacy and Search Removals FAQ, "What Are the Various Page Content Categories?" https://support.google.com/transparencyreport/ answer/7347822#zippy=%2Chow-do-you-classify-page-content%2Cwhat-

are-the-various-page-content-categories%2Cwhat-are-the-various-requester-categories%2Chow-do-you-classify-a-requester%2Cwhat-are-some-common-scenarios-where-you-do-not-delist-pages.

51 "Requested URL Delisting Rate by Category"; European Privacy and Search Removals FAQ, "What Are the Various Page Content Categories?"

52 According to the UK government website's explanation, "Under the Rehabilitation of Offenders Act 1974 (ROA), eligible convictions or cautions become 'spent' after a specified period of time, known as the 'rehabilitation period'." These "spent" convictions no longer need to be disclosed. https://www.gov.uk/guidance/rehabilitation-periods.

53 The remaining quotations and examples in this section are taken from the "Explore requests" section of the "Requests to delist content under European privacy law" page (i.e. Google's RTBF transparency report). The examples are tabulated in such a way that it is not possible to refer to them by any more precise identifier, as one has to simply keep clicking "next" to see another batch of five to six requests and cannot navigate to specific pages of requests directly. For each request, the summary of the request, the decision, and the reasoning were entered into a spreadsheet manually by the author to facilitate later navigation.

54 Kristie Byrum, *The European Right to be Forgotten: The First Amendment Enemy*. Lanham, MD: Lexington Books (2018), xvii.

55 Samuel W. Royston, "The Right to be Forgotten: Comparing U.S. and European Approaches." *St. Mary's Law Journal* 48.2 (2017), 253–75, 273.

56 Jack Balkin, "Free Speech in the Algorithmic Society: Big Data, Private Governance, and New School Speech Regulation." *University of California, Davis Law Review* 51 (2018), 1149, 1207.

57 Keller, "The Right Tools," 331–32.

58 Jeffrey Toobin, "The Solace of Oblivion," *The New Yorker*, September 2014. https://www.newyorker.com/magazine/2014/09/29/solace-oblivion.

59 Clay Calvert, "Fake News, Free Speech, & the Third-Person Effect: I'm No Fool, But Others Are," *Wake Forest Law Review* 52.1 (2017). http://www.wakeforestlawreview.com/2017/02/fake-news-free-speech-the-third-person-effect-im-no-fool-but-others-are/.
    The "direct causal link" standard comes from the 2011 case of *Brown v. Entertainment Merchants Association*, which struck down a California law that restricted the sale of violent video games to minors on the grounds that the law amounted to a content-based restriction and California had failed to demonstrate a "direct causal link" between the harm it sought to prevent and the restrictions, thus failing strict scrutiny. See *Brown v. Entm't Merchs. Ass'n*, 564 U.S. 786 (2011).

60 David Kaye, *Speech Police*. New York: Columbia Global Reports (2019), 101.

61 *Miami Herald v. Tornillo*, 418 U.S. 241(1974), 258.

62 James Grimmelman, Speech Engines. 98 *Minnesota Law Review* 868 (2014), 912.

63 See Grimmelman, Speech Engines, 929–31.

64 Quoted in Grimmelman, Speech Engines, 911.

65 Zhang et al. v. Baidu, 10 F.Supp.3d 433 (S.D. NY 2014), 438.

66 Google, Inc. v. Hood, 96 F.Supp.3d 584 (S.D. MS 2015), 598.

67 Electronic Frontier Foundation, Brief for the Plaintiff as Amicus Curiae, *Netchoice v. Moody*, United States District Court For The Northern District Of Florida, Civil Action No. 4:21-cv-00220-RH-MAF, 2021, 9–10. https://www.eff.org/document/amicus-brief-44.

4 Remedies
Reputation Management Practices

This chapter analyzes the work of reputation management, interrogating the degree to which it functions as a "right to be forgotten by other means" in more granular depth. As explained in the introduction, the construction of "reputation management" used here is capacious, encompassing any endeavor that is intended to improve how an entity – whether a business or individual – looks to those who encounter information about them online. The empirical analysis of the chapter is then broken into three segments.

The first speaks to the goals of reputation management by analyzing the ways in which reputation management professionals' self-descriptions in interviews and promotional materials published on the web characterize the kinds of things that they try to help with. The chapter then addresses a natural follow-up query: by what methods do they try to do this? Specifically, the same sources of interview and promotional data revealed a loose tripartite typology of the tactics used: efforts to affect the composition of search results through search engine optimization, efforts to either negotiate with the publishers or hosts of materials deemed to be harmful (including direct use of platforms' own terms of use), and tactics that use legal procedures in novel ways. Each of these two segments of the chapter discusses both goals and tactics that are described as "best practices" by professionals in the field as well as those which are perceived to be less reputable (or simply ineffective). Each section also assesses both the ethical principles that guide these endeavors and considers their ultimate impact on the marketplace of ideas.

Operationalizing Reputationally Damaging Material and Calibrating the Goals of Reputation Management

This section provides a textual analysis (based on collected web materials as well as interviews) that seeks to answer some basic questions

DOI: 10.4324/9781003287384-5

about how reputation management services are pitched as a "solution" to particular kinds of reputationally "problematic" speech. What do the people offering services to bolster your online reputation talk about the threats that they are there to help combat? What kinds of speech content do they claim they will help you with? Further, how do they frame the intended outcome of such endeavors? If we think of the question in terms of a generic reputation mad lib – i.e. "We work to [verb] the [noun] that is harming your reputation online" – what do those offering reputation management services seem to commonly place in the blanks?

One of the central takeaways from a comprehensive examination of the kinds of language used in promoting reputation management services is that the framing of the reputationally harmful content they pledge to ostensibly help clients deal with treats false, hyperbolically emotive, true but unflattering, and simply opinionated speech as fungible members of an all-encompassing category of "negative content." The kinds of results that exemplify this category vary somewhat. The company Overnight Reputation promises to deal with "online negativity," warning that the results can be "devastating" when "an individual or business has any less than flattering information online."[1] The CEO of a company called Cyberset, Shahab Saba, describes in a press release from 2018 how the need for reputation management addresses situations like "when professionals have a negative incident in the past – such as a lawsuit – that will turn up in searches and which have the potential to scare off potential clients or customers."[2] J. Wilson Advisers expands the category to include some interestingly specific content, describing how they "help organizations and individuals through reputational challenges, ranging from data breaches to financial crisis to #metoo moments."[3]

Walter Halicki, the CEO of ReputationMaxx (a company that appeared with disproportionate frequency in the NexisUni data used for this analysis) describes the target of his services as "unfavorable material," a category which encompasses "negative reviews regarding the service delivered by a person, unfavorable press released by a publication, and even inappropriate content posted on social media."[4] Elsewhere, he implores job applicants to remain vigilant about content that "show[s] that person in a negative light," because if such content were to appear in a search, he says (speaking as the hypothetical employer in the scenario) that "[he] probably wouldn't even call them in for an interview."[5] Shifting tone slightly, Halicki addresses another promotional document to "victims of online harassment" whom he will "help recover their positive online existence." While such people presumably lack any kind of culpability in their predicament, "a search result page full of negativity will deter uninformed customers who may think the information is legitimate."[6]

Overall, Adam Petrilli of the company NetReputation underscored in his written interview responses how "negative" is often in the eye of the beholder when it comes to the content that clients seek help with from reputation management services: "What may be negative to others not always is so obviously negative to another," he explained, and thus the targeted content may include

> [u]nwanted content, public records, negative news article, bad consumer reviews, negative opinion of a business left by a former employee, a political opinion someone doesn't agree with, unwanted photos, divorce records, bankruptcy records, arrest records, lawsuit documents, malpractice suit reports, SEC violations and much more.

Shannon Wilkinson of Reputation Communications likewise describes how a wide range of reputationally harmful content that might continue to plague someone through its presence online even if it is nominally true: these include "legal notices on high-ranking sites (references to lawsuits, divorces or similar events" as well as "[m]edia articles that do not present them in an accurate or current light."

Further, sometimes the content that clients want help with is not even "negative" per se; it simply impedes their personal reinvention, as was captured by the journalist Lauren Goode in her account of the "digital ghost" of her cancelled wedding from Chapter 2. Sometimes people find themselves in such a situation simply due to their proximity to notorious events. For instance, in an interview, Kent Campbell of the company ReputationX described a scenario involving a college student who had been wounded in a mass shooting. This student "came to us to change their narrative online," because "the person didn't want Google to associate them with being a shooting victim for the rest of their life."

Sometimes in descriptions of what the "negative content" category encompasses, reputation management professionals tend to lead with descriptions of legally actionable speech like "defamation" and "fraud" that are then mixed with the more varied descriptions of various "negative" results like those detailed above. This linguistic tendency rhetorically frames these kinds of "negative" content as illegitimately injurious in the same way as, say, "defamation" is, and thus by extension, marks it as equally deserving of erasure. A company called

Profile Defenders, for instance, describes how they will help to counter "negative reviews that are either outwardly false or misleading," and later ends up simply characterizing the material their clients seek help with as their "unwanted listings." But these categories of speech are of course dissimilar in their legitimacy: "outwardly false" speech is very possibly subject to legal action, while "unwanted listings" could encompass any number of things that otherwise contribute to the marketplace of ideas. Another company called Torati Consulting outlines a range of speech classifications that its services target. Their website describes the service as "help[ing] people and businesses repair unflattering, defamatory or otherwise damaging search results." Whether "unflattering," otherwise damaging," or "defamatory," the company implies, the remedy and the urgency with which it must be pursued are the same.

J.W. Maxx's CEO Halicki exhibits a similar tendency to combine references to defamation with other types of content. In describing his agency's approach, he refers once to the content being targeted as "negative content" and then subsequently as "slander."[7] The reference to "slander" implies that the "negative content" being displaced is illegitimate and perhaps even actionable, and thus suggests that reputation management services are perhaps being framed here as a solution to the unwieldiness or ineffectiveness of defamation law in the digital age. Yet elsewhere, it seems clear that the kind of image cleanup being proposed is much more capacious: in characterizing the "unfavorable material" that "can be grounds for a complete rejection of a job applicant," the company lists "negative reviews regarding the service delivered by a person, unfavorable press released by a publication, and even inappropriate content posted on social media."[8] So, while these might indeed sometimes represent the sort of content that is not actionable but still unduly harmful given its prominence (and that is ostensibly addressed in a reform like the Right to Be Forgotten), the linguistic framing also suggests that the kind of content these services really target is not confined to the rhetorically charged terms like "slander" and "defamation" that they use in headlines to convey illegitimacy. In fact, a company that calls itself Defamation Defenders outright nonetheless goes on to clarify that it actually addresses much more than defamation: "As part of personal reputation management projects," states their website, they have helped clients to combat "all types of negative website content from websites and internet search engines: images, blog posts, news articles, comments, etc."[9]

Yet this tendency is not necessarily the product of rhetorical sleight of hand or a promiscuous disregard for the relative value of different kinds of speech in the marketplace of ideas. Rather, some of those engaged in this kind of work emphasize how reckoning with the reputational risks of the digital age requires a more flexible understanding of what kind of content is "harmful" and perhaps warrants some kind of intervention. Dorrian Horsey, an attorney at the Minc Law Firm, described how at bottom, her and her colleagues' essential service is to "help people solve problems regarding content on the internet," and this can be in situations where perhaps "it's content that someone has posted about you that is false, or maybe it's something that was published about you that was true, but it's in some way harming your reputation." Regarding the latter scenario of true content harming someone's reputation, though, Horsey and her colleague Andrew Stebbins were clear to frame the justification for intervention by describing a hypothetical client who is experiencing precisely the kind of "stuck in time" phenomenon described in Chapter 2:

> Every time their name is searched on the internet, this incident or this report comes up, and while the rest of the world has moved on and is concerned with other things, that person is stuck there because they can't get past that moment in time.

This rhetorical implication of a kind of deservingness on the part of the client who seeks to minimize the visibility of particular "negative" but true content related to their name was also conveyed in a number of explicit characterizations offered by digital marketing and reputation management professionals in conversation and in their promotional web materials. While promotional descriptions of the services may sometimes exhibit a tendency to lump together categories of content that are actually very different, it is also clear that many of these professionals operate with a genuine conviction that they are helping people to restore a kind of control over their image that has been unfairly stripped away. Mike Munter, who runs his own company in the Pacific Northwest that provides a number of digital marketing and search engine optimization services, emphasized in our interview that an important impetus for his work is that he "fundamentally believes that every individual and business has the opportunity to protect [them] self" given the ease with which reputations can be maligned online. He repeatedly characterized the ostensible beneficiary of services like his as people who seek help "so that they can move on in their lives." And as the aforementioned Profile Defenders puts it straightforwardly on its website, "[l]arge corporations, small businesses, individuals – everyone deserves the right to be represented fairly on the internet."[10]

In fact, some of the professionals who work in the reputation management sphere themselves express support for a reform in the style of the Right to Be Forgotten. This is unsurprising given their evidently common perception that reputations are unduly threatened in the digital age, but it is also somewhat surprising in the sense that legislation to this effect would seem to obviate some of their work. Shannon Wilkinson, for instance, asserted that she and the others at her firm "are advocates for privacy protection and the 'Right to Be Forgotten' on Google," and she added that she thought "[e]veryone should be." Others like attorney Kenton Hutcherson expressed support in theory, but simply thought it would not pass constitutional muster in the United States. As Hutcherson put it, while he "sees some utility" in its approach, he reasoned that it was "not feasible... based on our values and the rights that we have in the Constitution."

There are several specific types of online sources that show up repeatedly in these professionals' descriptions of the unfair predicaments that they seek to help clients with and in general promotions for reputation services online. Each embodies a distinct aspect of the ways in which online platforms and online information sources with potentially productive uses have also – perhaps inadvertently – ended up creating disproportionate reputational harm. These are: mugshot websites and other digital traces of criminal records, and various platforms for user-generated reviews, most notably so-called "gripe" platforms which are intended to give anonymous posters the opportunity to call out both interpersonal and commercial transgressions ranging from adultery to poor customer service to fraud. It is important to introduce these sources of content in some depth here, as they are targeted with particular reputation management methods that will be discussed in the following section.

What distinguishes "gripe" sites and the related constellation of what we might call "callout" platforms from more commonly known review platforms like Yelp or Google Reviews is twofold. First, they are largely unmoderated. Second, their own linguistic framing of the kind of content they host seems to encourage a particular kind of vengefulness. The tagline of Ripoff Report, possibly the most notorious gripe site, for instance, is "don't let them get away with it." Other sites announce a similar kind of orientation in their names themselves, of which some examples are Dating Psychos, The Dirty, Exposing Johns, and Cheater Registry – though it is worth noting that the traffic on these more niche sites is likely much smaller. Ripoff Report disclaims any attempt to actively screen and filter out the crude or false statements from the eloquent or true statements. The colorful founder and self-described "Ed-itor" of Ripoff Report, Ed Magedson, explicitly contrasts his approach with that of other consumer sites. His own website characterizes him as someone who "has one goal in mind — to empower consumers by helping them speak out."[11] Gripe and other "callout" sites therefore represent an online niche where information seekers can find an unadulterated glimpse of the unvarnished opinions and experiences of the public.

Postings on these sites are a frequent target of reputation management services. Reputation professionals sometimes cast them as the epitome of the kind of unduly damaging but also generally not very productive or valuable speech that plagues their otherwise honest, sympathetic clients. Mike Munter, for instance, described the backwardness of the situation this way:

> you can go on there right now and write a story about how I screwed you and you can totally make it up and now all of a sudden I Google myself and I see Ripoff Report page one, and there's no editorial review.

Both journalists and scholars have also been sounding the alarm on mugshot websites for some time. Generally, the moniker refers to "online photo galleries [that]...are based entirely on [mugshots] already available from local police departments."[12] Yet they represent precisely the kind of decontextualized personal information discussed as such a prevalent source of risk in Chapter 2, as "they often do not tell the whole story, including who was ultimately convicted or who had had charges dropped."[13] Communication and legal scholar Mark Grabowski has provided a comprehensive overview of the criticisms and justifications that circulate regarding this type of content as well as the unlikelihood of finding recourse in legal action. He notes that while some in journalism defend the practice of posting this information on the grounds that "the public not only has a right to know but demands to know as a matter of safety."[14] On the other hand, "[c]ritics argue mugshot galleries are more voyeurism than journalism: by allowing readers to view neighbors, colleagues, and acquaintances in embarrassing situations, the sites pander like trashy supermarket tabloids to society's sordid interest in gossip and sensational crime stories."[15] Grabowski quotes a Salt Lake City defense attorney named Ken Yengic's criticism of the sites as creating undue harm without adding meaningfully to the marketplace of ideas: "It does not add anything to the public debate about crime and how we deal with crime...it just gives the citizenry at large a way to make fun of people."[16] Despite this, their content is almost certainly constitutionally protected as long as the arrest information contained in the posts is indeed accurate.[17]

Reputation management professionals often explicitly reference mugshots and criminal records in promoting their services. The company Swiftly Labs, for instance, that "[i]f you have been arrested in the USA or Canada, chances are your busted mugshot can be found online if someone searches for your name on Google or other search engines," and this is a problem because "your troubled past can affect your life."[18] Like in Grabowski's account, they specifically address those who might have been " wrongfully arrested and charged," as "even if you were innocent, and or [sic] the charges dropped or dismissed, your mugshot can still be found online." Their appeal, then, is for prospective clients to "simply contact us and we will get your arrest mugshot taken down from any website that has it" instead of "having your life turn into a nightmare." The company quotes a price of $189 and a turnaround time of a few days for the work to be done.

Another company called Internet Reputation provides a concurring characterization of the work, claiming that "[a] publically available mugshot can be devastating to a reputation, but [they] can remove them quickly." The company in fact characterizes mugshot issues as a kind of "gateway" to more comprehensive reputation management, as they also describe how in a specific case they "were perfectly capable of providing these clients with an immediate response that could remove negative information, [but] we wanted to stick with them and build a firewall for them, so they wouldn't be attacked in the future."[19] As recently as 2019, a company called, simply, Remove My Mugshot created a service that is framed in explicitly self-help terms: so that "[m]ugshot victims can avoid paying hundreds or thousands of dollars in fees to erase mugshots, which can be republished on different websites the guaranteed-removal companies own," they "created a step-by-step blueprint on personal reputation management and made it available as a download for $39.99."[20]

Practical Remedies for Reputationally Damaging Speech Online

These last characterizations of the kind of content that is targeted in reputation management also introduces us to some of the language that is commonly used about what is, ideally, to be *done* to such content. This section covers the three main methods of reputation management practices: search engine optimization, negotiation with content creators and hosts, and strategies that leverage the content policies of platforms. While the practices themselves are the focus (both in terms of their efficacy and ethics), these sections also take particular care to attend to the linguistic patterns that are evident in the descriptions of such practices.

Search Engine Optimization

Search engine optimization (SEO) is arguably the most fundamental practice in the toolkit of reputation management. More precisely, though, the work that goes into enhancing the online reputation of a particular entity (whether a person or a business) represents a particular SEO challenge. The marketing website *Moz* defines the overall endeavor of search engine optimization as "the practice of increasing the quantity and quality of traffic to your website through organic search engine results."[21] In practice, then, the goal of SEO is to boost the visibility of the entity in question in ranking for particular search keywords. So, the role of SEO in reputation management can be thought of as the attempt to make the composition of the results returned for a very particular keyword (the person's name, for instance) reflect most favorably on that person. Sometimes the threshold task is to first get the results to include links that have to do with the person in question at all (say, if it's a common name). In other cases – such as the highly publicized instances where a relatively obscure individual experiences a moment of online notoriety that becomes, in Michael Fertik's words earlier, "the only thing the internet thinks about you" – the task is of course to affect the composition of those results so that they reflect a more comprehensive portrait of the person.

Google and other search engines are something of a "black box," and they constantly tweak the ways in which their search algorithms weigh different criteria in determining what results to return for particular queries. Nonetheless, they also do provide some transparency in how the algorithms work and what people can do in order to maximize the visibility of web pages. The website Search Engine Land – one of the leading sources for news and information about search engines on the web – has outlined the basic criteria for optimizing a website's performance in search results.

Search Engine Land breaks the factors first into two fundamental categories: "on-page" and "off-page" attributes. On-page refers to aspects of the website itself. Search Engine Land describes the page's content itself, for instance, as "the cornerstone of your SEO efforts," noting that search engines reward pages that provide "substantive, useful and unique" content and effectively integrate the keywords for which your site will (theoretically) be a useful result in a search.[22] Aspects of the site's architecture and html code are also important on-page factors. These include, respectively, things like the navigability of pages and speed with which they load, and the ways in which the site's html code maximizes the way a search engine can "understand" what the page is about through things like titles and headings. Off-page criteria involve things that will affect search results composition that are external to a website, such as links pointing to it, its reputation, and attributes of the user who has entered the search terms. Links to a site have been long regarded as the equivalent of a "vote" in favor of that page, signaling to the search engine that someone else considered the page useful enough to connect its readers to it.[23] Yet the specific source of the links matters too: for instance, "[a] link from a news publication with a strong journalistic reputation is going to be more valuable than a link in the comments section of a blog that has nothing to do with your industry."[24]

In general, both search engines and SEO professionals stress that it is counterproductive to attempt to game the algorithm to include a page in results for a particular search query when it is not actually relevant or useful. In other words, a major element of the "common sense" on which the industry is built seems to hold that search engine results generally *do* more or less elevate the pages that most substantively and effectively "answer" the searcher's query and demotes results that are a poor fit, especially those that have tried to misrepresent themselves off as relevant and useful. Google itself (and presumably other search engines) in fact can significantly demote sites if it detects actions that it perceives to be attempts to trick it. Search Engine Land explains, for instance, how SEO practitioners sometimes include an instruction in the code for a website that effectively tells the search engine not to "count" a link to another site for its search algorithm if the link appeared in a comments section.[25] Even though links are a source of information that can be useful for a search engine, writing a throwaway comment and placing a link to one's webpage at the bottom (often with a list of keywords as the hyperlink text) has also long been considered a kind of spam by Google. As the company itself explains, "[t]he best way to get other sites to create high-quality, relevant links to yours is to create unique, relevant content that can naturally gain popularity in the Internet community."[26] Because of the perceived importance of *not* appearing to try to trick Google, therefore, "[s]ome publishers went as far as to nofollow all outbound links in their content to avoid the appearance of being involved in link schemes."[27]

As implied in Google's explanation and stated outright in the Search Engine Land guide, a foundation of SEO involves the actual creation of the content that one wants to rank highly in searches for particular terms. A significant portion of the work of reputation management services, unsurprisingly then, focus on such content. While the verbs vary, perhaps the most common description of what these practitioners are trying to do in such cases is to "push down" search results that are putatively harming the client's reputation. Defamation Defender calls this general reputation management practice "reverse SEO," and describes how it endeavors to "bury" the negative by creating new content and "optimizing" the way that both this new content and existing content is perceived by search engines. The digital marketing professional Garrett Sussman clarified in an interview, however, that there is a limit to how much of an effect these SEO efforts can have on particular links depending on the source. He offered the example of how "trying to push down bad content with good isn't necessarily going to work if it's like an article from the New York Times – that has so much authority in search that it's probably never going to happen." This would appear to contrast with the outcomes that are obtainable through the RTBF's delisting decisions, therefore, as the prominence of the publication would presumably not stand in the way of delisting if the underlying content were deemed worthy of "forgetting."

Nonetheless, simply creating new content on particular platforms can definitely have an impact on the composition of the results pages. The aforementioned Defamation Defenders counsels "[s]tarting a blog and publishing engaging, helpful content on a regular basis[;] Publishing other types of content that position your company as an industry expert" such as "[w]hite papers, articles, and industry advice forums (like Quora)[; and generally] being active on social media, or starting a new social media channel."[28] Popular social media sites, in particular, appear often in the list of suggestions, as they seem to rank well in searches quickly and the possibility of posts being shared can also multiply their reputational impact. The company Fishbat, for instance, asserts that

> [i]f a company isn't established on Facebook, Twitter, or LinkedIn, just to name a few examples, building an online reputation will be next to impossible...not only should these platforms be established early on, but they must be maintained with consistent posts, complete with information that's relevant to users.[29]

Another recurring point of basic advice is that it is important to write content that itself uses the key terms that are commonly referenced in the existing negative search results. Defamation Defenders, for instance, describes in a promotional blog post how a reputation SEO endeavor should "use the keywords that previously brought up results about your court case, arrest, or criminal record, and build them into positive content," because "[t]his way, Google is more likely to return positive content when people enter these search terms."[30] Halicki of JW Maxx similarly describes the firm's approach as "releasing positive content, and using the keywords in negative content to push the slander off of page one."[31] Peter Tosto, a digital marketing professional and the proprietor of a new platform called FindIt, provided a complementary description of the overall approach: "you have to see what words you're indexing for negatively, you create content around those same words that were used negatively about you [but] in a way that you want to be perceived."

One area of content creation that reputation management professionals counsel caution with, however, is direct counterspeech responses to the reputationally damaging material that clients seek to suppress. Kenton Hutcherson explained the careful approach that he recommends on this matter: while the circumstances of course vary, "if you are attacked online…in a negative forum like a place for negative reviews, you certainly do not want to engage in that forum." This is because "it can create more content for the search engine, so it makes it far more relevant, and it also can have the effect of legitimizing the conversation to other people." While perhaps common-sensical, a corollary principle, then, is that in the situations where responses will not hurt from an SEO perspective, the response must nonetheless still take the high road in the conflict. Halicki of JW Maxx, for instance, asserts that "an impulsive response can prove to be disastrous," because the respondent is "damaging their image as a respectable and level headed professional" and further, "will usually only bring the original instigator back for more."[32]

Practitioners seem to largely concur regarding content creation that attempts to game search engines by flooding the web with redundant, low-effort content mostly does not work anymore (at least not in a sustainable way), and that the best approach instead simply focuses on providing content that is useful, accurate, and labeled and organized effectively. Peter Tosto of FindIt, for instance, described in an interview how for all of the hand-wringing about how Google's algorithm tweaks might affect how well a site ranks, what matters far more is that the SEO practitioner is generally following best practices:

> when you go out and you create relevant content in writing with images, you title those images correctly, you put up a video and the video is relevant to what it is you're actually trying to get indexed

under, and you title that properly in YouTube, and you're not trying to fool anybody, this is gonna get indexed.

This attitude is further manifest in one particular framing of reputational SEO as a kind of storytelling that recurred in promotional materials and discussion with practitioners. Tony Wright, who runs the firm
Wright IMC, for instance, stresses that the real point of his service is
"telling your side of the story as well as promoting positive stories that
might otherwise go unnoticed." The implication, in other words, is that
the underlying objective of reputation management SEO is not simply hiding unflattering information. Instead, it is genuinely working to
contribute material that is consistent with the function of a search engine, which the digital marketer Sussman described succinctly as "present[ing] to you the best answer for whatever question you're asking."
As Wright continues, "[they] believe every company and individual has
a positive story to tell – whether they know it or not," and thus the objective is in fact to *enrich* the information-scape of search engine results
through content created and elevated through SEO.[33]

Other reputation management practitioners reinforce this kind of
framing in their representation of SEO as a method. The website for
the company Status Labs frames the value of SEO in terms of whether
the content is indeed useful for the user who is looking for information:
"the focus for content has shifted from keyword stuffing and writing
for search engines to thinking about the users reading your content,
and if you're answering their questions." This approach is important,
they explain, because search engines take the time spent on a page
into account as one indicator of "quality" in determining search result
rankings: "content that doesn't keep users on a page for long, or causes
them to leave without clicking through to another page on your site,
won't help your business or your ranking in search results."[34] Kent
Campbell of ReputationX also reinforced this point, describing how
what he called "dwell time" can help determine how Google decides
where to rank a site:

> In order for content to suppress or push down negative content
> people have to interact with it without 'bouncing' too much…[i]f a
> lot of people click on a headline in SERPs, then click back, it tells
> Google there is an issue with the content.

In contrast, according to Campbell, "[b]etter content is rewarded by
more clicks and higher 'dwell time' on the page…[e]ventually this content outranks the bad because it's better and more relevant."

Though the company is now defunct, Rich Gorman of Reputation Changer provides a complementary characterization of content building for reputational SEO as storytelling – in this case, about a business: "a company like Reputation Changer will seek to build a comprehensive narrative about the brand in question, highlighting all of its attributes and underscoring the things that make it uniquely desirable to consumers."[35] It is "[t]his positive, brand-enhancing narrative" that is what is ultimately successful in "suppress[ing] and replac[ing] any online listings or reviews that are less than favorable." Presumably, then, a business for which such a story could not authentically be told would simply fail to displace the negative results – which again theoretically frames the best practices of reputational SEO as providing an enrichment of the marketplace of ideas.

While reputation management professionals are often prevented from discussing the specifics of individual cases by confidentiality agreements, some anonymized and general examples give insight into the types of outcomes using these methods. In turn, they give us another concrete way to assess the impact on the marketplace of ideas. A company called Swiftly Labs describes one example involving a "famous rapper [who] was accused of criminal activities but was not convicted." The reputational injustice, as the company frames it, was that even after his acquittal, the search results for his name largely referenced the allegations rather than his exoneration. As a result, the company "worked with the rapper and his manager to…immediately weaken the rankings of the negative search results and bury them deep into the search engine results pages (SERPS) by promoting positive content online." The company reports having ultimately been "able to dominate the top 3 pages of search results with relevant and well thought off [sic] content in about 50 days."[36]

IC Media Direct also offers some examples of instances in which it endeavored to "Push Down [sic] undesirable search results," as they characterize it for potential clients on their website. The "before" screen capture of the first page of results for a client named Nick Kohlschreiber shows two gripe site postings alleging that he "scammed 51 employees." The first page of results is currently occupied mostly by profiles on major social media platforms (such as Twitter, LinkedIn, and Pinterest), several press releases on sites like Access Wire that host such user-generated content. These reference Kohlschreiber as a "traffic genius" and "media genius," and describe some of his professional work in the digital marketing industry and his company AccesSIO. Overall, they display the kind of informative – though perhaps somewhat generic – approach to writing promotional content that was described above as part of SEO best practices. The gripe site postings were also from 2010 to 2011, and one might therefore conclude that the newer, more uniformly positive search results page represents an outcome that is consistent with the ethos represented by the RTBF of untethering one's digital identity from the most scandalous (and possibly even false) material posted years prior.

Another example from IC Media is perhaps more dubious. The "before" search results page they display on their website for a client named Chris Kamberis lists several links pertaining to investigations and lawsuits about payday lending schemes run by Kamberis. In 2015, Kamberis agreed to pay $85,000 in restitution to the state of Arkansas, and a settlement was also reached with the Washington state Division of Consumer Affairs in late 2014, part of which required Kamberis and an associate to "not apply to the Department for any license under any name" for a period of five years following the date of the order. Indeed, perhaps to IC Media's credit, such links no longer appear on the first page of results for Kamberis' name. Aside from one link to the website of a Greek photographer with the same name, they instead now appear to be dominated by pages associated with his real estate company in Kansas City. These include several of his own websites and promotional press releases offering things like "tips on when to invest in property,"[37] related social media pages, as well as coverage of transactions in business news publications. The links therefore appear to again embody the kind of reputational restoration that contributes to the marketplace of ideas by providing both useful information and a more up-to-date reflection of the person's activities.

Yet there are also aspects of the new scenario that might give us pause. The nature of the transgressions that IC Media has ostensibly helped to direct attention away from might strike some as indicating serious moral turpitude. New York, for instance, has made payday lending illegal because it preys on financially desperate people while ultimately escalating their financial problems. "Payday loans are designed to trap borrowers in debt," according to the New York Department of Financial Services, "[as] due to the short term, most borrowers cannot afford to both repay the loan and pay their other important expenses."[38] Even if one endorses the notion that our digital identities should not be exclusively defined by our worst transgressions, should those transgressions not represent at least one part of the picture? The outcome for Kamberis here does seem consistent with Google's seemingly routine de-indexing of prior legal issues in response to RTBF requests provided that the person in question seemed to have turned a corner in life, but the passage of time in this particular case might also strike one as insufficient for the payday loan settlements to be truly irrelevant.

Further, while the content that currently comprises page one of the results certainly appears superficially substantive, the picture becomes more complicated once we scratch the surface. On Kamberis' CTK real estate website, for instance, the "clients" page displays corporate logos for some of the most recognizable companies in the world, such as Shell, Burger King, and McDonalds. Several of them contain hyperlinks to something that is labeled a "client letter." The documents that these links direct to, however, are confusing in that they appear to be reference letters from individuals employed at the company in question, not an indication of a "client" relationship within the ordinary meaning of that word.[39] Additionally, the signatories of the letters have a limited digital presence themselves: for the McDonalds and Burger King referees, for instance, the only seemingly relevant digital footprint is a LinkedIn page that contains a relatively small number of connections and very little in the way of additional professional information. Even if these "client letters" are in fact authentic, one might wonder what exactly they add that would be of value to interested parties seeking information about the company's business record.

Some other case studies in which the client is simply described in terms of their general identity and their problem also provide insight into the ways in which search engine optimization campaigns address reputational issues that are out of reach of the law. Internet Reputation details one involving a "successful businessman with multiple franchises" who "found records of a legal case that had been filed against him [that were] appearing as the first result on Google, meaning anyone who searched for his name would see this unwanted, damaging information." The company claims that the impact was severe, as "several acquisitions fell through due to those searches, and the client found that his reputation within the business community was greatly diminished." Its approach to remedying the situation involved a "customized plan which included numerous digital assets such as websites, blogs, press releases and professionally written content, highlighting his positive assets." Although the company only describes their approach to elevating the search position of these content "assets" in general terms, the result was evidently the "suppression of the unfavorable assets," which they later claim "effectively removed the unfavorable assets from the first page of Google results."[40] As with the Kamberis example, therefore, the net result seems to be a kind of erasure similar to that offered by the RTBF. The impact of this "record of a legal case that had been filed against him" could have indeed been disproportionately harsh for the individual in question, but we are again left to wonder if *some* trace of the issue might not be warranted even if it is rightfully counterbalanced by a more comprehensive portrait of this individual's other successes.

The company VelSEOity explains a case study on their website that illustrates how the SEO approach can help address the presence of "gripe" site postings as well. The content at issue in this case was a Ripoff Report posting that "suggested that the client had a poor service [sic] and though there were significant inaccuracies that weren't even related to the client's business in the Ripoff Report, the site refused to remove it" (as readers will recall is typical of appeals to gripe sites for removal). The client was experiencing reputational harm from even this one posting because "[t]he Ripoff Report ranked third for the client's brand when searched for on Google." VelSEOity's approach, therefore, was "to push it out of view in the search engine results out of sight for potential customers," which specifically meant simply "off the first page of results."

They did so through a specific approach to content creation and linking. First, they explain how they created the typical "variety of branded written and video content for the client in the form of interviews, Q&As and other positive content." To optimize it further, part of the added value they describe providing was that they "added this content to a variety of well chosen, relevant and powerful media sites that we have relationships with," and they more deeply associated this content with the client's online identity by "promot[ing] it with a mixture of link building and social media via the client's social media accounts." The impact of this, claims the company, was that the client "received significant SEO boosts from links with the articles back to their site," and thus the Ripoff Report posting is "now on page 3 of the SERPs for the branded term and does not impact on the seller's reputation."[41]

Overall, therefore, this situation appears to show reputation management SEO being used in a manner that is less at odds with the marketplace of ideas. A Ripoff Report posting containing derogatory opinions perhaps does not represent the kind of essential information that an official document from a legal settlement does in the first place. Further, if there were indeed factual inaccuracies in the posting then pushing it off of the first page of results essentially represents a more efficient (and indeed even plausible) solution in lieu of a legal mandate to compel removal. Finally, while the RoR posting is no longer among the most conspicuously displayed pieces of information about the client, it is still relatively easy to find.

Yet in the case of Ripoff Report and other gripe sites, at least, there also appears to have been a change in the way Google's search algorithm weighs their authority in search results. Mike Munter explained how he typically refers inquiries about gripe site postings to specialists, as "it's a pretty big niche," but in the last few years, he has generally received fewer calls about such content to begin with. His interpretation of the reason is that "Google took some kind of manual action because it used to rank highly [and] it 'doesn't rank as well anymore... based on the number of calls we get." Kenton Hutcherson concurred that "Google changed how strongly Ripoff Report appears in search results," and more specifically dated the beginning of this change to "around November of 2018." During our interview, Peter Tosto of FindIt searched to see whether Ripoff Report links still appeared in the results for a prior client of his, and concluded that he "think[s] what [Google] has probably done over the years is maybe reduce the value of the relevancy of this content...maybe they 'don't treat it as trustworthy as other content about someone." In fact, based on how infrequently he hears about the site now compared to years past, Tosto was surprised that I had asked about it and wondered "if [it was] even around anymore."

What this all reinforces, ultimately, is the position of Google as one of the central arbiters of what is or is not known (or one might even say knowable) about a person in the digital age. Its decisions about how to calibrate its search algorithm are hugely consequential in terms of which results are favored or disfavored for particular search queries. Munter described its function in this vein as "making decisions about what does need to be known till about somebody and what maybe 'doesn't."

Some search experts and reputation management practitioners perceive Google itself to have become more genuinely sensitive to its power and responsibilities as an intermediary. Barry Schwartz, an editor at Search Engine Land, has explained how sites that involve medical or financial advice – or what the publication cheekily calls the "your money, your life" niche – are now "particularly scrutinized" for their credibility. He paraphrased Google's comment on the issue in the following way: "Google said, 'Hey, if we're going to recommend this content to people, we need to make sure it's trustworthy, authoritative and an expert's writing it.'"[42] Kenton Hutcherson suggested that Google's evolving treatment of sites like Ripoff Report likewise reflects and increasing willingness to reckon with its role in amplifying particular sources of information that are repeatedly singled out as a scourge in the marketplace of ideas:

I think that companies like Google have started to recognize that their approach of being neutral, trying to remain neutral, opened the door to a lot of very abusive behavior, and for people that have been victims of internet defamation, 'they've been trying to bring this issue up for years and years and years.

He credits current events and general awareness of the issue as the impetus, explaining that "'it's finally coming to the mainstream attention because of what happened in the [2016] election and 'what's happened in terms of the polarization of society."

Others take a more skeptical view. To Kent Campbell of ReputationX, while Google and other major platform intermediaries are indeed "the arbiters of truth in today's society," he portrays them as more agnostic with respect to the impact of the information they foreground. In contrast with a hypothetical situation he described in which moderators determine that a particular piece of information should clearly remain tied to a person's digital identity because they could pose a danger to others, he says that "Google doesn't do that...[i]t simply displays information based on its popularity and perceived relevance to the query. It doesn't care if it's ruining someone's life."

In this situation – where Google (and other search engines) act as "arbiters of truth" yet do not necessarily "care if [they're] ruining someone's life" – then, what other options are available to those for whom working to affect the composition of search results through SEO is either insufficient or not expeditious enough? The next section explores different approaches that seek the modification or removal of reputationally damaging content itself that have been embraced in the absence of a Right to Be Forgotten in the United States.

Content Modification and Removal

The approaches discussed in this section can be split into two subtypes, each of which seeks to have content actually changed or removed rather than simply repositioned in search results. The first of these subcategories involves appeals for the removal of content based on platforms' own terms of use. Sometimes these procedures can be completed by the aggrieved party themselves, though reputation management services also work to spread awareness of their availability and help clients navigate them in some circumstances. In other cases, the platform terms themselves necessitate the execution of specific legal procedures as a prerequisite, and this set of tactics thus again highlights how legal and public relations services are sometimes inextricable in the overall endeavor of reputation management. The other subcategory involves negotiation with creators and content proprietors directly. Sometimes this approach is again undertaken in a DIY fashion, but reputation management professionals again also provide guidance and specialized savviness in navigating the negotiation, and certain publications have even ended up altering their overall policies on requests for content removal at the behest of these professionals.

In their promotional materials, reputation management services describe the possibilities for removing content in a tone that can at times sound immodest and even censorial in spirit (though the companies are not instruments of the state and thus do not "censor" in the technical sense, of course). The company Profile Defenders, for instance, boast of their "sophisticated techniques [that] allow our clients to get rid of their unwanted listings." In another pitch, Profile Defenders simply proclaims that it can "get negative results completely erased from the internet" – a claim which is supported by a testimonial from a "Fortune 500 CEO" who was amazed that "[t]he bad result is 100% gone not just hidden." This kind of language seems to cut against the manner in which SEO is presented as simply telling the client's (arguably more relevant) side of the story, as it instead frames success in terms of whether "the bad result is 100% gone." Even if the claims are stated less ostentatiously, it is nonetheless common to see references to content being "removed" in reputation management promotional materials. Ultimately, the appetite for content "removal" to which these companies are ostensibly responding is symptomatic of a more general popular desire to reclaim some form of control over one's digital image. As law professor Eric Goldman suggested in a blog post about a reputation management company that had sent him a baseless demand to remove content from his blog, "some folks desperately want a magic wand that would allow them to remove online discussions about them at their discretion...[n]o such magic wand exists, but plenty of businesses are happy to peddle the dream."[43]

Other professionals are quick to counsel modesty in promoting what they can do for clients. Shannon Wilkinson, the CEO of Reputation Communications, unequivocally rejects the kind of language on display in the Profile Defenders example: "[w]e do not mislead the public into believing that they can 'wipe away' unwanted Internet results by hiring us, or any firm. We do not use words like 'suppress' or 'whitewash' when we describe our services." In fact, Wilkinson was deliberate in characterizing what her company does as "[u]pdating search results" – a description much more in line with the ethos of "everyone has a positive story to tell" expressed by Tony Wright in the previous section – and emphasized that doing so "is usually a long, painstaking process." Yelp's blog likewise warns business owners about the inflated claims of some in the industry: "[t]here are dozens of 'reputation management' companies that claim to work with Yelp to remove your negative reviews or otherwise boost your ratings for a fee," but if a business is "wondering how these companies can make good on this offer, the answer is simple: they 'can't."[44]

That said, there are particular circumstances in which professionals working the reputation management realm do indeed provide something akin to "removal." Overall, these practices often hinge on the policies of some of the biggest intermediaries regarding the removal of particular content if presented with a valid court order establishing that it violates the law. This method is often employed in order to deal with gripe site content. As readers will recall from earlier in the chapter, one of the central features of gripe sites is their intransigence when it comes to content moderation. Even if content is found to be defamatory, Section 230 protects them from liability if it was submitted by a third party and the site did not meaningfully contribute to the creation of it (under the Roommates/Accusearch line of case law interpreting Section 230). The Seventh Circuit decided a case in 2010 which determined that RoR's refusal to remove postings despite a default injunction obtained by a victim of defamatory postings on the site did not constitute "active concert and participation" with the anonymous users who created the postings.[45] Further, the site can even refuse to remove postings if the original poster requests it out of contrition. This had led to situations where, as Florida's Third District Court of Appeals has put it, "[e]ven when…a user regrets what she has posted and takes every effort to retract it, Xcentric [RoR's official company name] refuses to allow it," and it is fully within its legal rights to do so because it "enjoys complete immunity from any action brought against it as a result of the postings of third party users of its website."[46]

While the posts may never be removed from RoR, then, they can still be effectively rendered invisible to most people if Google does not index them. As summarized by the company Reputation Rhino, Google's stated policy is that it "will remove a post from search results after being presented with a court order that determines the content to be false and defamatory." This approach is thus useful both in situations where the content host refuses to remove the content as well as situations where the poster's identity remains unknown, thus thwarting direct litigation.

In our interview, Andrew Stebbins and Dorrian Horsey of the Minc Law Firm provided a comprehensive overview of the process that they go through in order to help clients get content removed from search results. They start by "fil[ing] a 'John Doe' lawsuit [meaning the identity of the defendant is unknown] against the anonymous reviewer," and then "send out subpoenas to whatever platform that review or the statement or the website host...to get data associated with those accounts on log out IP addresses that were used for those logins and the account creation." With this information in hand, they then can "search and find out which internet service provider services those IP addresses," and after convincing the relevant court to issue a subpoena to the internet service provider, they "most of the time will come back with an identity for at least the account that the reviewer used to publish that account."

In this interim stage, it appears that the Minc Firm also enters comments on gripe site postings indicating that a lawsuit has been filed, that the poster "may have a right to file and serve a response to the subpoena anonymously," and providing contact information and a deadline by which the poster must do so.[47] While there is of course a practical reason for doing so, the practice also represents an interesting extension of an observation that has been made about the function of defamation lawsuits for businesses in the digital era. As Kishanthi Parella has written, "corporations file lawsuits in response to unfavorable online reviews in order to send a message to the public, refuting the allegations, and to investors, assuring them that the corporation is stable."[48] In this particular case, while the comment on the posting plays a procedural role in the lawsuit, it also serves an informational function for the public.

In the subsequent stage of the court proceedings, sometimes they are not able to obtain an actual identity or even an account name, such as when the poster was "using a proxy server or Tor browser" or "if the data is expired or for some reason one of either the Internet service provider or the platform 'doesn't have data." In this event, they "move for... either a default or a summary judgment against the defendant." Though such a motion will typically succeed against an absentee defendant who does not provide an answer on their own behalf, the Minc attorneys stressed the importance in this situation of actually presenting evidence to the judge considering the motion to establish that the content in question does in fact constitute defamation or some other legal wrong, as the platforms evaluating requests for content removal are unlikely to be satisfied with a mere default judgment entered because the defendant failed to show up to contest the allegations. Stebbins thus explained that in accordance with this policy, they go through and put together affidavits and outline all the reasons why we think that this is either a fake review, not left by a real customer or a competitor or whatever the reason is, and we present all of that evidence to the court in order to get a judgment.

To complete the process, finally, "once we have that judgment on the back end 'that's looked at evidence and had things considered, we can take that to the platform, and most of the time were successful in getting them to take down the content."

The process now appears to be well established. A variety of companies in the constellation of reputation management practitioners beyond those that are law firms make reference to it in their promotional materials, such as Reputation Rhino (a company that simply labels itself a "top-rated Online Reputation Management [sic] company"), which describes its services as "creating and optimizing positive Internet content and/or assisting with court-ordered removal."[49] It is important to point out, though, that the relative standardization of the tactic appears to have evolved out of experimentation. The website for Kenton Hutcherson's law firm describes how Hutcherson's 2011 article detailing the approach actually galvanized Google to create a more standardized procedure: once the article "detailed the then-secret removal technique," the result was that "[a]pproximately two weeks later, Google launched an online portal to receive court order and removal requests."[50]

On a conceptual level, what is most significant about this approach is that while it engages the civil legal process, it does so with the primary objective of simply removing the content (and in a secondary sense, communicating to the public that the defamatory statements have been challenged in court prior to the resolution), not obtaining damages or some other vindication against the perpetrator. As Stebbins emphasized, "the cases in which we actually collect money for our clients are few and far between, [so] the main goal needs to be taking down the content, getting it removed from the internet." As a corollary, therefore, this means that the decision is still ultimately the intermediary's to make; the court order essentially functions as a tool of persuasion, not compulsion per se. This outcome seems to align with the reformulation of the goals of libel law suggested by the reformers covered in Chapter 1. While the studies associated with the Annenberg Libel Reform Project (discussed in Chapter 1) did find that plaintiffs were sometimes motivated by "vengeance," the overarching concern was simply establishing the truth and clearing their name. It would appear that the removal method pursued via court order on display here aligns with the reformers' findings, as it offers a remedy that simply addresses the practical harm being done by the content involved instead of rectifying the situation through financial compensation. Further, it is at least partly consistent with the mechanisms of the RTBF – with a key difference, of course, being that there is no data protection authority to whom the individual seeking delisting can appeal a denial by the search engine.

Unfortunately, there are a number of unscrupulous approaches to reputation management using legal tools that have also cropped up in recent years. In particular, the well-regarded technology blog Techdirt and the legal scholars Eric Goldman, Eugene Volokh, and Paul Alan Levy have been instrumental in bringing these schemes to light. While the fact that they have been exposed has presumably led them to be discontinued, they nonetheless reflect the way in which the imperative of achieving reputational "justice" given the precariousness of reputation in the digital age can be taken to overzealous extremes that detract from the legitimate endeavors to help people without undermining the marketplace of ideas.

The first of these schemes builds off of the court order process described above. Along with Levy, Volokh discovered in 2017 that a company called Solvera Defendants – which also did business using monikers like "Instant Complaint Removal" and "DefamationRemoval.com" – was offering a service that promised to remove postings from review websites. To do so, it engaged in a version of the court order removal process, in which it would contract with an attorney to file a defamation lawsuit against the purported poster of the offending content, who had signed an affidavit agreeing that they had made the posts in question. When a judgment invariably comes against the defendant, Solvera then presents it to Google to convince it to delist the links in question. The problem, however, was (at least) twofold. First, the defendants named in the lawsuits were simply confederates of the company who had adopted the role of "defendant" under the pretext that they had added additional postings to the original content in dispute, whose original author of course remained unknown. Though they had only authored the additional postings, the affidavits stipulated that they admitted to being the authors of the initial postings as well. Second, Solvera had misrepresented the situation to both its customers and to local attorneys in Northern California who actually filed the cases, who were unaware that the "defendants" were fake and did not in fact even reside in the correct jurisdiction.[51]

Another method documented during the summer of 2017 involves what researchers at Lumen referred to as the "stolen article scam," the general approach of which "uses fake websites and backdated articles to remove content online" by leveraging platforms' policies regarding the removal of content that infringes intellectual property rights.[52] As described by Lumen researcher Mostafa El Manzalawy, the perpetrators of this technique start by creating a website that masquerades as a journalistic outlet, copying real journalistic content from other sources around the web, and then backdating the content on the newly created website to make it appear that the genuine news articles were in fact plagiarized from the site created by the reputation management outfit. The reputation management companies would then avail themselves of the well-established mechanisms for requesting that content be delisted or removed outright because it constitutes an intellectual property infringement that are common across Google, other platforms, and legitimate journalistic outlets.

Using Google's transparency reports, publicly available website domain registration data, and various services such as the "Wayback Machine" that archive historical snapshots of particular web addresses, El Manzalawy offers the example of an entity calling itself "Fox 18 News Network LLC" to illustrate an instance in which the scam apparently worked. In 2016, the company issued a DMCA takedown notice regarding an article that had been published in the New York Daily News in the fall of 2014. The evidence of "infringement" that it submitted was a copy of the same story dated one day earlier than the story was published by the Daily News. The problem, however, was that the website domain registration information available shows that the company did not even operate the URL until 2015, and further, the various page archives show no actual content on the page until 2016, when it seems safe to infer that the copied "infringing" article was actually published by Fox 18 News Network LLC. The Lumen study indicates at least 52 instances of takedown requests fitting this pattern since 2013, with around 30% of them successfully resulting in delistings.

Practices that deceptively leverage the removal policies of the platforms are simply a more recent iteration of the kinds of disreputable (or what are sometimes referred to as "black hat") approaches to reputation management that have long chagrined the more established practitioners in the industry. In Nora Draper's discussions with reputation management professionals Patrick Ambron (of the company Brand Yourself), Michael Fertik (of the pioneering Reputation Defender), and Chris Martin (of Reputation Hawk), each expressed frustration at the ways in which, as Fertik put it, "some of [the companies] are run by very dastardly people."[53] Draper further speculates that it is perhaps the "desire to avoid being lumped in with the 'bad' industry players" that explains their hesitation to recognize a broader "industry" of reputation management to begin with.[54] Buzzfeed News published a long article in 2019 detailing some of these less reputable tactics, such as creating online "alter-egos," or fake personae using a client's name so as to divert attention from whatever negative search results, and, perhaps humorously, the creation of essentially fake scholarships (in that there are likely no actual recipients) that get listed on prestigious universities' websites, which often have high authority in search results. Andy Beal, a marketing expert cited earlier, is quoted in the article as unequivocally declaring such practices as "examples of the 'black hat, unethical techniques' that have emerged in the industry."[55]

Yet while these kinds of practices undoubtedly cut against the claim that reputation management can provide a more seemingly legitimate redemptive function for those experiencing disproportionate reputational injury without polluting the marketplace of ideas, the article also asserts that it is "difficult to tell the good guys from the bad guys" in the world of reputation management. As per Beal's comment above, this ignores the areas in which there does appear to be a relative consensus among many practitioners about what best practices look like and how to approach the question of which clients to work with in the first place. Even though there are, demonstrably, practitioners who do utilize some of the less reputable techniques described above, others express skepticism about their efficacy in addition to misgivings about their ethical validity. Kent Campbell of ReputationX explained that his firm eschews these kinds of diversionary SEO tactics because they do not actually help clients in the long run:

> Why not just publish a bunch of junk content? Because it doesn't work (and could harm our clients). Most "online reputation management companies" use what we call a "spray and pray" approach. They publish a lot of spun content (computers write it) or just junk (non-native content creators). This tactic used to work, but no longer does. Sadly most people don't know that.

Garrett Sussman echoed this sentiment, suggesting that such tactics "do[n't] really work as much anymore because Google's a lot smarter."[56] Marketing strategist Susan Bird has described how "she is constantly asked by clients to flood their online review listings with positive reviews, but says she always turns them down," as not only is it a "highly unethical practice," it is one that "will sooner or later catch up to the business" even if it works in the short run.[57] Sussman was also unequivocal in framing fake reviews on a client's own behalf as being firmly in the "black hat" category of practices that any reputable service will eschew. Indeed, this seems logical enough, as along with the removal schemes described above that relied on fabricated defendants, they are largely tantamount to fraud.

While it is harder to ascertain a consensus regarding the ethical parameters for selecting clients, recurring themes did surface in the interviews and promotional materials. Some practitioners appear to have considered the issue more than others, but even those who stress their lack of categorical restrictions on whom they work with nonetheless clarified particular types of content they would not help to suppress. For instance, when asked if there were particular types of clients that he would not work with, Adam Petrilli of NetReputation responded in the negative, emphasizing that "[they] are a business and [they] operate without prejudice." Yet despite this overall orientation, he also subsequently added that they "do turn away violent or sexual crime related offenders."

Other interviewees expressed a range of attitudes regarding their particular categorical boundaries. Garrett Sussman specified that he had "seen agencies who are not comfortable working with the gambling industry, the pornography industry, the substance abuse industries, [and the] pharmaceutical industry." Kenton Hutcherson described situations in which his firm has "had some political groups approach us for things have been said about them, and sometimes when you get into extremist groups... we tend to stay out of that." While he clarified that this was "not to say that it would be unethical to represent them" for anyone per se, it was not his "preference in that type of situation." Shannon Wilkinson offered "information about criminal behavior, including any actions that have harmed the public and are a matter of public record" as examples of information that reputation management professionals should not help to suppress.

Contrastingly, Kent Campbell expressed reservation about the permanence of even such information. He argues that while it is of course reasonable to expect search results to contain a (metaphorical) "warning sign on a fence that says 'dog bites'" because "people have a right to know before they walk into the yard," he also wondered rhetorically whether "the fact that someone went to prison [should] hang around in search results forever keeping that person from attaining gainful employment."[58] To him, this result can be "akin to a life sentence." Overall, he stressed the fact that often "it's a tough call" and that decisions need to be evaluated on a case-by-case basis. In his own practice, Garrett Sussman explained that because he is "all about inclusivity and stand[s] against racism and prejudice...it would be hard for [him] personally to ever work with a client who had committed crimes that [he didn't] agree with." (He did also add cheekily that he "probably wouldn't work with a murderer.")

Horsey and Stebbins of the Minc firm offered a similar perspective on the need to thoroughly consider the implications of each individual case through one's own moral compass. Stebbins offered an example of a past client who came to the firm for help with search results pertaining to a sexual assault conviction He elaborated on his thought process in evaluating the decision:

> When the consult came in, I was like, okay, this is pretty questionable...I don't know if I feel comfortable taking this kind of case. But then I talked to the guy, I was able to get some more information...[and] there were certain extenuating circumstances that led me to believe 'okay, I understand. You admitted to this...' he served his sentence and he would like a fresh start.

It was because he went through this detailed consideration, therefore, that Stebbins was able to conclude in this particular case that "getting this new story removed is a way to help him, but not something that's compromising my morals." In other words, instead of some kind of categorical policy about whether they will or will not take clients with sexual abuse convictions, the decision will be based on their own case-by-case evaluation of the public costs of rendering information less visible.

Interestingly, none of the practitioners explicitly offered commentary in one direction or another on the status of either government officials or people who are highly influential in society – what tort law calls "public figures" – within this ethical calculus.[59] Yet the underlying principle that emerges from their responses is that they clearly find it important to portray the clients they accept as, in some way, *deserving* of help. This tendency also lays the groundwork for the final dimension of practice, that of negotiation and direct interpersonal appeals for removal. Deservingness is the cornerstone of the rhetorical appeal in this context, and the overall pitch might be summed up by the phrase "sometimes it is *right* to allow something to be forgotten, even in the absence of an official '*Right* to Be Forgotten.'"[60]

In some sense, discussing this more interpersonal dimension of reputation management here is akin to ending at the beginning. Many accounts of the process from professionals start with a suggestion that the aggrieved simply reach out to whomever might be responsible for posting (or at least hosting) the content, explain the harm it is causing them, and request that it be either removed or modified. Reputation Rhino begins its advice with the stipulation that they "we first recommend contacting that website's owner, content provider, or domain provider," as "[i]f successful, this will remove the content at the source."[61] In their interview responses, Kent Campbell and Adam Petrilli each indicated that moving on to a consideration of SEO or possibly legal approaches only happened after first exploring whether the publisher would remove the content if asked. On their blog, Campbell's company ReputationX elaborates further, explaining that while voluntary removal is not granted often, it does *sometimes* happen. They suggest trying to ascertain what would motivate the publisher or author to remove the content, and they list donations to charities and even direct payment as ways in which they have negotiated removal.[62]

On the other hand, just as attempts to game the content removal mechanisms have surfaced in recent years, the direct negotiation approach is also sometimes carried out in a boorish – if also often impotent – fashion. In the earlier example of the legally dubious takedown request received by law professor and blogger Eric Goldman, for instance, he noted that the company was charging $140 for the questionable service, when "[a]t no cost to the sender, [he] could have just as easily rejected a takedown notice sent directly to [him]."[63] A series of articles from 2015 in Techdirt, likewise, chronicles the belligerence of a "reputation management bro" – as they put it – named Patrick Zarelli.[64] The conflict started because Zarelli "was hired by an attorney named Gary Ostrow to 'clean up' his Google mentions." To do so, Zarelli apparently

> seem[ed] to think that the proper strategy to 'manage' Ostrow's Reputation' was to call up a bunch of these lawyers — many of whom have built their reputations on protecting free speech rights — and threatening them, saying they should take down their blog posts.[65]

As the post noted, the result was simply that "[l]ots of people wrote about Zarelli's fuck up, including us." Such an anecdote therefore highlights how the wrong approach to negotiating content removal can actually result in *more* (legitimate) reputational damage, as it risks triggering what Techdirt's Masnick has famously labeled the "Streisand Effect," or the "online phenomenon in which an attempt to hide or remove information…results in the greater spread of the information in question."[66]

Perhaps unsurprisingly, some of the legal practitioners in the reputation management sphere exemplify a more professional orientation toward negotiation as a means of obviating the more drawn out process of pursuing a lawsuit. The attorneys at Hinch Newman, for instance, proudly describe on their website how they have "had numerous posts containing defamatory, false, or misleading comments 'voluntarily' removed by the website owner or 'anonymous' poster, without the need to resort to formal litigation."[67] Horsey and Stebbins of the Minc firm spoke at length about the importance of sometimes first approaching content publishers with an appeal intended to stimulate empathy for their client rather than present a legal ultimatum. While offering the caveat that they are of course lawyers and thus they fundamentally view their work through that lens, Horsey described how at the end of the day, "our primary focus is helping our clients remove content from the internet in a variety of circumstances, so…sometimes we are wearing a more persuasive hat." Like in the framing from ReputationX above, she stressed the importance of feeling out what kind of appeal a particular content host will be most receptive to.

More specifically, both offered commentary on an extended hypothetical that dealt with how they might approach negotiation with a news publication. In those situations, issuing legal demands is "the exact opposite of what is going to be most effective because they are more educated in the First Amendment, and they're not afraid of being sued." Instead, an appeal that concedes that the publication is under no mandate to comply but appeals to their empathetic side can be more effective. As Horsey put it, this approach involves "coming in with a more editorial approach to say, 'here are the reasons why this is continuing to cause harm to my clients'" and explaining how the publication can justify the decision to remove or alter content without compromising its own mission of providing newsworthy information to the public. She called this "humanizing the client" by detailing the disproportionate impact that the visibility of the information is having on their life. Ultimately, the goal is to assuage the publication's reasonable skepticism, because it is understandable if the natural response of a journalist might be "[w]hy should we take something like this down if this person is a threat to society?" She thus emphasized that "you have to answer that question for them," but that if you do, then sometimes they are receptive.

That said, even the somewhat optimistic commentary from Horsey and Stebbins still acknowledged the default recalcitrance of journalistic outlets when it comes to removal of true content. Others in the reputation management sphere are even more emphatic on this point. Defamation Defenders' web pages on removing various types of content describe how "[w]riters and editors of newspapers and magazines feel as though their articles make up the public record," and thus "many publishers have rules against unpublishing old content, stating that they will not rewrite history."[68] Further, some empirical research suggests that appeals to empathy are not likely to be sufficient: in a survey of 110 Canadian journalists and editors, they report, "not one would remove content based on simple remorse or embarrassment on behalf of the person in the article."[69]

Yet there is also some indication that this attitude may be changing. Horsey and Stebbins explained that we are in the midst of a significant shift in the orientation of journalistic outlets toward modification and even removal of content. Horsey described how there has been change in the receptiveness of editors and publishers she negotiates for removal with, as she has "been here long enough now that [she has] gone back to publications that originally said no and got a yes." She attributes at least some of this to personnel turnover, where "[m]aybe one person said no, and then a couple of years later, the next person says, 'oh, I see this a little differently...yeah, we'll take it down.'" A current impediment is still that "often they are empathetic and sympathetic to the situation our clients find themselves in, but they don't want to move beyond whatever their stated policy is for that type of content." Nonetheless, her sense from conversations with people in the industry is that

> [at] some of these larger media corporations that have policies of not removing, there are many folks that are talking about this behind the scenes and trying to determine 'what is our policy going to be for our particular company, and can we move and make some adjustments to help people so that they can get relief?'

Overall, she forecasts that "the future is moving more in the direction of helping people who find themselves with this type of content online and are trying to find a way to remove it."

As they also pointed out, this "future" has in some sense already arrived given the initiative of some publications to rewrite their removal policies for specific situations. The *Cleveland Plain Dealer* has been a leader in this area. In 2018, they announced a policy explicitly modeled after the notion of a "right to be forgotten" through which "people can ask to have their names removed from old stories about minor crimes they committed." And while they do also address the role of the notion of "deservingness" that provided an implicit rhetorical ground-ing for some of the advocates of negotiation cited above, their criteria are modeled more directly on the legal procedure of obtaining record expungement. As they explain, [p]eople who have committed nonvio-lent crimes who successfully petition the courts to permanently delete all records of their criminal cases will be able to send us a request, along with proof of the expungement, and in most cases, we will re-move their names from the stories about them on cleveland.com." As a result of this, correspondingly, "Google searches of their names will stop finding those stories."[70] At the same time, the publication has also carved out exceptions for "elected officials, celebrities and other public officials," as well as violent or sex crimes." It thus partially mirrors the logic of defamation law in recognizing a greater interest in discussion of public figures, and also channels some of the ethos advocated by the reputation management professionals who designated information about serious crimes to be beyond the purview of legitimate reputation management.

The company Patch, which runs a network of hyperlocal news sites, has developed a similar policy with regard to particular situations in which a story about an arrest was published but the person was eventu-ally exonerated. Like the Cleveland example above, they require "doc-umentation from the court, the arresting police department or your attorney (with a signature and letterhead)...[t]o show charges are no longer valid."[71] They also recognize that an important component of relief in these situations involves the visibility in search results, and thus will also send a request to Google to remove your name from search results [so that] a search for your name no longer results in a link to the article."

The *Plain Dealer* has also taken steps to modify the way they ap-proach the inclusion of identifying personal details in crime reporting. This change is first grounded in a reformulation of the parameters of "newsworthiness." In the announcement of the new policy, the authors reflect at length on exactly the kind of disproportionate visibility of mug shots that we have thus far seen lamented widely by commenta-tors on the reputational dynamics of the internet. More specifically, they pledge to be more judicious in determining whether there is true news value in naming individuals who are the subject of crime stories. Outside of these cases, however, they have decided to "stop naming most people accused of most minor crimes." And in terms of the use of photographs in crime stories, the publication has also decided that it will simply "go to the court appearance and shoot our own photo" in the event that they "believe news value exists in a photo of an accused criminal." Overall, their use of mug shots will thus be "greatly curtailed, [and] restrict[ed] to the most notorious of crimes."

There is some indication that these internal policy changes are becoming more widespread as well. In early 2021, the Michigan news portal MLive publicized its evolving orientation toward what it called the "growing phenomenon...of individuals who have been the subjects of news coverage ask[ing] to have those stories removed." Kelly Frick, Senior News Director of the site, was quoted outlining how they will now approach such cases: though

> MLive doesn't have a formal set of guidelines, nor software tools, to proactively find all old content that might merit review [as the article notes that Cleveland.com is working with Google to do], they still "do welcome take-down requests, and each one is reviewed thoroughly by Frick and relevant editors before a decision is made.[72]

While they too stipulate that certain content will not be removed in various circumstances, such as when it seems necessary to "protect the public" or when they feel they "need to keep [the content] as a part of the record for a community," the goal is to incorporate conscious reflection on the long-term effects of a story on its subjects into editorial decisions. As Frick characterizes it, this involves asking themselves "[h]ow is this going to be perceived a year from now, or five years from now? Is this story important enough to write about it in this particular way?" Again, the specific language in these descriptions echoes the criteria considered in the Right to Be Forgotten – namely, the degree to which a story continues to be relevant years after it was first published, and whether the disproportionate impact its visibility is having on its subject outweighs the newsworthiness of the information.

Finally, reputation management professionals also publish much material online that is ostensibly promotional but offers genuine guidance on the various possible avenues of obtaining content removal. Much of this effort focuses on raising awareness about removal mechanisms outlined in platform content policies that members of the general public can utilize without court documents. Andrew Stebbins described how prospective clients will sometimes approach the Minc firm because they want to see personal information removed from personal information aggregator websites such as MyLife.com, and the firm will often simply instruct these prospective clients on how to utilize the sites' own procedures for requesting the removal of personal information. Likewise, Shannon Wilkinson emphasized that there "is substantial, free 'how-to' information provided by online reputation firms like [Reputation Communications]."

One particular category that has emerged recently is Google's procedure to "remove content about me on sites with exploitative removal practices from Google" – though this is itself merely one of the sub-categories of "personal information" removal that Google has offered for some time.[73] Google describes these particular sites as "sites that require people to pay money directly to the sites or to other agencies to get the content removed," and some have suggested that this is meant to encompass sites like Ripoff Report.[74] The procedure simply asks requesters to fill out a form where they indicate that the content is about them, demonstrate (e.g. via screen capture) where it is on the website, and explain why the site fits the above definition of "exploitative removal practices." One of the preliminary screens does also ask the requester if they have asked directly for the content to be removed and offers to help figure out how to do so, but does not prevent a request from being generated based on the answer to this question. Overall, this can be seen as another aspect of the evolution in voluntary removal practices that concede to long-mounting pressure for the major platforms to help ordinary people deal with the reputational fallout caused by specific types of internet content.

Notes

1 http://overnightreputation.com/history/.
2 "Shahab Saba and Cyberset Say That Reputation Management Tips Highlight Why Professional Support Is Often Essential." *PR Web*, May 22, 2018. https://www.prweb.com/releases/2018/06/prweb15527445.htm.
3 https://jwilsonadvisors.com/.
4 "Why Job Seekers Are Finding Better Results with Proper Online Reputation Management." *PR Newswire*, July 29, 2014. https://advance.lexis.com/api/document?collection=news&id=urn:contentItem:5CST-GGJ1-DXKS-J4R6-00000-00&context=1516831.
5 J.W. Maxx, "Online Reputation Management Techniques: DIY Ways Individuals can Protect Their Online Image from JW Maxx Solutions." *PR Newswire*, May 22, 2014. https://www.prnewswire.com/news-releases/online-reputation-management-techniques-diy-ways-individuals-can-protect-their-online-image-from-jw-maxx-solutions-260273361.html.
6 "Online Reputation Management Expert Warns of the Dangers of "Anonymous" Internet Defamation." *PR Newswire*, May 7, 2013. https://advance.lexis.com/api/document?collection=news&id=urn:contentItem:58C8-JH61-JB4P-V3F9-00000-00&context=1516831.
7 "Reputation Management Agency JW Maxx Solutions Offers Effective Methods For Removing Internet Defamation." *PR Newswire*, March 19, 2013. https://advance.lexis.com/api/document?collection=news&id=urn:contentItem:580V-0171-JB4P-V2NB-00000-00&context=1516831.

8 "Why Job Seekers Are Finding Better Results with Proper Online Reputation Management." https://advance.lexis.com/api/document?collection=news&id=urn:contentItem:5CST-GGJ1-DXKS-J4R6-00000-00&context=1516831.

9 https://defamationdefenders.com/reputation-management/personal/.

10 "Profile Defenders – The Worldwide Leader in the Online Reputation Management Services Industry Succeed Where Others Fail." *PR Newswire*, February 29, 2012. https://advance.lexis.com/api/document?collection=news&id=urn:contentItem:5 52Y-BH21-F18Y-Y0RT-00000-00&context=1516831.

11 "Did You Know?" edmagedson.com.

12 Mark Grabowski, "To Post or Not to Post: The Ethics of Mugshot Websites." *Journal of Media Law and Ethics* 8.2 (2020), 21–36, 22. http://law.ubalt.edu/academics/publications/medialaw/pdfs_only/Vol.%208%20 No.%202%20002.pdf.

13 Grabowski, *Journal of Media Law and Ethics*, 22.

14 Grabowski, *Journal of Media Law and Ethics*, 22.

15 Grabowski, *Journal of Media Law and Ethics*, 24.

16 Grabowski, *Journal of Media Law and Ethics*, 25.

17 Grabowski, *Journal of Media Law and Ethics*, 22.

18 Swiftly Labs, "Remove Online Criminal Records & Mugshots." n.d. https://www.swiftlylabs.com/remove-online-criminal-record?fbclid=I-wAR0FXWMTCNIeykGjZcyvQ4MVb2R1DaWgPzLuvTicvT4_k84jf-miS6McHWWk.

19 "InternetReputation.com Awarded Highest Client Retention Rate in the Industry." *PR Newswire*, June 28, 2013. https://advance.lexis.com/api/document?collection=news&id=urn:contentItem:5 8SC-16J1-DXKS-J361-00000-00&context=1516831.

20 "New Reputation Management Course for Mugshot Removal." *Newswire*, August 27, 2019. https://www.newswire.com/news/new-reputation-management-course-for-mugshot-removal-20976281.

21 "SEO 101." *Moz*, n.d. Available at: https://moz.com/beginners-guide-to-seo/why-search-engine-marketing-is-necessary.

22 "Chapter 2: Content & Search Engine Success Factors." *Search Engine Land*, n.d. https://searchengineland.com/guide/seo/content-search-engine-ranking.

23 "Chapter 6: Link Building & Ranking in Search Engines." *Search Engine Land*, n.d. https://searchengineland.com/guide/seo/link-building-ranking-search-engines.

24 "Chapter 6."

25 "Chapter 6."

26 "Link Schemes." *Google Search Central*, n.d. https://developers.google.com/search/docs/advanced/guidelines/link-schemes.

27 "Chapter 6."

28 "How to Repair Online Reputation Damage with Reverse SEO in 2021." n.d. https://defamationdefenders.com/blog/reverse-seo-reputation-repair/.

29 "New York Social Media Agency, Fishbat, Discusses How Companies can Use Online Reputation Management to Showcase Corporate Social Responsibility." *PR Newswire*, August 9, 2019. https://yhoo.it/2YUHy47.

30 "How to Remove Court Cases from Google and the Internet." n.d. https://defamationdefenders.com/blog/how-to-remove-court-cases/.

31 "JW Maxx Solutions Offers Effective Methods for Removing Internet Defamation."

32 "Online Reputation Management Techniques: DIY Ways Individuals can Protect Their Online Image from JW Maxx Solutions."

33 "Online Reputation Management Services in Dallas." n.d. https://wrightimc.com/our-services/reputation-management/.

34 "SEO Content Strategy: How to Write Articles That Rank." n.d. https://statuslabs.com/content-strategy/.

35 https://en.wikipedia.org/wiki/Brand.com.

36 "Online Reputation Management (ORM) Case Studies." n.d. https://www.swiftlylabs.com/online-reputation-case-studies.

37 "Chris Kamberis – CTK Real Estate Offers Tips on When to Invest in Property." *WBOC*, July 24, 2021. https://www.wboc.com/story/44369477/chris-kamberis-ctk-real-estate-offers-tips-on-when-to-invest-in-property.

38 NY State Dept. of Financial Services, "Predatory Loans and Loan Scams." n.d. https://www.dfs.ny.gov/consumers/banking_money/avoiding_predatory_loans_and_loan_scams.

39 See, e.g. https://www.ctkrealestate.com/wp-content/uploads/mcd_letter.pdf and https://www.ctkrealestate.com/wp-content/uploads/bk_letter.pdf.

40 "Reputation Management Case Studies." n.d. https://www.internetreputation.com/case-studies.

41 "Case Study 2." n.d. https://velseoity.com/case-studies/654-2/.

42 "Chapter 5: Trust, Authority & Search Rankings." *Search Engine Land*, n.d. https://searchengineland.com/guide/seo/trust-authority-search-rankings.

43 Eric Goldman, "Doing Online Reputation Management? Don't Do It This Way." *Forbes*, May 14, 2015. https://www.forbes.com/sites/ericgoldman/2015/05/14/doing-online-reputation-management-dont-do-it-this-way/?sh=6d6bd5605b86.

44 "What's the Deal with Those Companies That Claim to be Able to Help Me Manage My Reputation on Yelp?" *Yelp Support Center*, n.d. https://www.yelp-support.com/article/What-s-the-deal-with-those-companies-that-claim-to-be-able-to-help-me-manage-my-reputation-on-Yelp?l=en_US.

45 Eric Goldman, "Ripoff Report Isn't Bound by Injunction against User Post–Blockowicz v. Williams." *Technology and Marketing Law Blog*, December 28, 2010. https://blog.ericgoldman.org/archives/2010/12/ripoff_report_d.htm.

46 Quoting *Giordano v. Romeo*, 76 So. 3d 1100 – Fla: Dist. Court of Appeals, 3rd Dist., 2011. Aaron Minc, "Ripoff Report: A Deep Dive into the Site, Lawsuits, & Getting Removed." August 31, 2017. https://www.minclaw.com/ripoff-report/.

47 See, e.g. the comment from "mincllc" filed in response to the following RoR posting: https://www.ripoffreport.com/report/jamila-jaffal-abraham-ameena/north-olmsted-cleveland-parma-1483776.

48 Kishanthi Parella, "Public Relations Litigation." *Vanderbilt Law Review* 72 (2019), 1285, 1288. https://wp0.vanderbilt.edu/lawreview/2019/05/public-relations-litigation/.

49 https://www.reputationrhino.com/homepage; https://www.reputation-rhino.com/our-solutions/ripoffreport-removal/.

50 https://hutchersonlaw.com/about/.

51 The summary here is paraphrased from: Tim Cushing, "Texas Attorney General Issues Complaint Against Reputation Management Company for Bogus Lawsuits." *Techdirt*, September 13, 2017. https://www.techdirt.com/articles/20170912/15434738200/texas-attorney-general-issues-complaint-against-reputation-management-company-bogus-lawsuits.shtml.

52 Mostafa El Manzalawy, "Data from the Lumen Database Highlights How Companies Use Fake Websites and Backdated Articles to Censor Google's Search Results." August 24, 2017. https://lumendatabase.org/blog_entries/800.

53 Nora Draper, *The Identity Trade*. New York: NYU Press (2019), 152.

54 Draper, *Identity Trade*, 153.

55 Craig Silversmith, "How to Game Google to Make Negative Results Disappear." *Buzzfeed*, June 27, 2019. https://www.buzzfeednews.com/article/craigsilverman/google-search-manipulation-online-reputation-expert.

56 The following can perhaps serve as an instructive, though not conclusive, illustration. In a video from 2010, Daniel Cohen offers a reputation management demonstration where he finds a random announcement of a crime on a district attorney's website and then "saturate[s] the internet with tens or hundreds of thousands of results for the purposes of flushing these negative results to the end of the search engine." While he does show an "after" results page that appears to reflect success, one of the first comments on the video points out that the results related to the crime were back on the first page for the same name query days later. This is true of the current composition of the results as well (screen capture available). https://www.youtube.com/watch?v=nfP2eIGxMfU.

57 SEODagger, "Expert Exposes Shady Reputation Management Companies." *MarketersMedia News Hub*, September 22, 2016. https://advance.lexis.com/api/document?collection=news&id=urn:contentItem:5KS7-VH8 1-F03R-N2DT-00000-00&context=1516831.

58 For what it's worth, Campbell also supplied the following in regard to the evaluation of potential clients at the company:

> [e]very prospective Reputation X client is vetted by the team. With the exception of the CMO (Kent Campbell) the entire executive team is female, are all mothers, and are all over 40. I mention that because I believe it colors the types of clients we accept.

59 Kent Campbell of ReputationX did seem to address potential clients who have achieved some kind of negative notoriety in the public eye, however, stating that: "horrific acts and trending content with a lot of momentum cannot be 'fixed' and often shouldn't be. If a company causes a problem in a community, the community should know about it."

60 I am indebted to Dr. Paul Siegel for suggesting this phrasing in his feedback on a manuscript that I submitted while he was editor of *First Amendment Studies*.

61 "Remove Negative Search Results." n.d. https://www.reputationrhino.com/our-solutions/remove-search-results/.

62 Kent Campbell, "How to Delete Something from the Internet." September 1, 2021. https://blog.reputationx.com/how-to-get-online-content-removed#ask.

63 Goldman, "Doing Online Reputation Management? Don't Do It This Way."

64 Mike Masnick, "Florida Bar Laughs Off Nonsensical 'Bar Complaint' by Reputation Management Bro Patrick Zarrelli." *Techdirt*, December 2, 2015. https://www.techdirt.com/articles/20151201/23575332963/florida-bar-laughs-off-nonsensical-bar-complaint-reputation-management-bro-patrick-zarrelli.shtml.
65 Masnick, "Florida Bar Laughs Off Complaint."
66 Mario Cacciottolo, "The Streisand Effect: When Censorship Backfires." *BBC News*, June 15, 2012. https://www.bbc.com/news/uk-18458567.
67 https://www.hinchnewman.com/practice-areas/internet-law/internet-defamation-and-online-libel/.
68 "From Published to Unpublished: How to Remove Arrest Articles from the Internet." n.d. https://defamationdefenders.com/blog/how-to-remove-articles-from-internet/; "How to Remove Court Cases from Google and the Internet," n.d.https://defamationdefenders.com/blog/how-to-remove-court-cases/.
69 "From Published to Unpublished."
70 Chris Quinn, "Right to be Forgotten: Cleveland.com Rolls Out Process to Remove Mug Shots, Names from Dated Stories about Minor Crimes." *Cleveland.com*, July 12, 2018. https://www.cleveland.com/opinion/2018/07/right_to_be_forgotten_clevelan.html.
71 Geoff Dempsey, "How to Remove Your Information from Patch." July 15, 2021. https://patch.com/us/across-america/how-remove-your-information-patch.
72 John Hiner, "The Internet Never Forgets or Forgives, and That's Why MLive Considers Requests to Remove Old Content." *MLive*, January 7, 2021. https://www.mlive.com/news/2021/01/letter-from-the-editor-the-internet-never-forgets-or-forgives-and-thats-why-mlive-considers-requests-to-remove-old-content.html.
73 https://support.google.com/websearch/answer/9172218?hl=en.
74 See, e.g. Kashmir Hill, "A Vast Web of Vengeance." *New York Times*, February 2, 2021. https://www.nytimes.com/2021/01/30/technology/change-my-google-results.html.

Conclusion

There is widespread agreement that the internet has brought about reputational threats that were minimized in previous technological environments due to the way their architecture afforded a number of built-in, default mechanisms for "forgetting" information about a particular person. Popular discourse on the issue typically contrasts the approach taken in the EU via the Right to Be Forgotten with the absence of a single sweeping legal reform in the United States. This is of course sensible on one level, of course, as structurally they are indeed very different. Yet the contrast is smaller when we consider how the diverse endeavors of reputation management provide a supplementary restorative force for reputational "justice" that is not wholly dissimilar from the outcomes that are in evidence in the European context.

In terms of its tangible impact on the marketplace of ideas, the RTBF appears to have had a fairly modest impact thus far. Based on the prevailing interpretation of the new GDPR mandates for data controllers, Google and others have significant latitude to determine how to operationalize deliberately broad mandates to determine things like "the seriousness of the interference with the data subject's fundamental rights to privacy" in its decisions about whether to delist a link. And based on the publicly available record of its decisions thus far, it appears that Google – the entity with perhaps the *greatest* incentive to represent the situation as one in which the public is being deprived of critical information – has interpreted its mandates in a way that fairly consistently adheres to a few rules of thumb. It delists links in situations involving individuals who were charged but not convicted of a crime, situations in which it determines that an individual has essentially "moved on" sufficiently from whatever professional or personal activity the search results currently still reflect, and instances in which "sensitive" personal information is contained in the link. While there is also some evidence that the company has been somewhat lenient in removing links

DOI: 10.4324/9781003287384-6

that relate to involve serious crimes or other improprieties committed by an individual, there is room for debate about the propriety of such decisions on a case-by-case basis; one cannot conclude categorically that the public is being deprived of crucial information in order to mitigate the reputational consequences for undeserving data subjects.

The professionals who contribute to reputation management often operate in a way that mirrors both the impetus for and execution of the Right to Be Forgotten. First, their work is conceived in a way that is consistent with – rather than antithetical to, as one might initially expect – the importance placed in public relations ethics on advocacy that contributes to the marketplace of ideas, as well as the core principle in the Supreme Court's defamation and privacy jurisprudence that reputation protection should not compromise an "uninhibited, robust, and wide-open" public discourse. We can observe a consistently articulated hegemonic ethos regarding redemption and reputational justice in reputation management discourse, and this is evident from their descriptions of the reputational threats experienced by ordinary people, the role that their services play, and the kinds of people they are trying to help.

Their practices often – though not always – result in outcomes that are also similar to those generated by the Right to Be Forgotten. The search engine optimization work that they perform often has the effect of adjusting the balance of information about people's lives that is most prominently visible online. Likewise, tactics that leverage the removal policies of the major platforms and Google – whether using legal procedure or simply documenting how the content in question violates the platforms' terms – also provide a means of dealing with recurrently problematic sources of content (e.g. mugshot and gripe sites) that do not technically run afoul of existing law. And it is perhaps due in part to the influence of reputation management advocacy that both the platforms and content publishers have evolved in their orientation toward removal of content based on appeals grounded in the rhetoric of personal redemption that undergirds the spirit of the Right to Be Forgotten as well. All in all, the outcomes often parallel those of Google's EU delistings: people who demonstrate that they are being impeded in their personal growth and livelihood and demonstrate sufficient "deservingness" – whether through personal development, extenuating circumstances, or both – are afforded the opportunity for their digital identities to "move on" just as they have in their personal lives.

While the likelihood that comprehensive legislation modeled on the European Right to Be Forgotten would be viable in the United States is small, therefore, supporters of such a change can take some solace in the supplementary function that "private ordering" appears to be playing. To be sure, reputation management practices *do* reflect the kind of neoliberal worldview that many critical scholars disdain for good reason. In leaving solutions to the private sphere of "self-help" and excusing the seemingly inexorable decline of public resources and support, it undoubtedly results in those with greater resources enjoying disproportionate benefit. Yet encouraging this approach also appears to accord with the positive dimensions of self-help discussed in Chapter 1. As we have seen, the endeavors that are being pursued in reputation management also increasingly involve cooperation and assistance from the platforms and publishers themselves, and thus promote "republican virtue" through more direct, sometimes even informal settlement of disputes. Likewise, this conversation has arguably galvanized an evolution in cultural and professional norms around what is considered "newsworthy" and how individuals' past transgressions should be judged. Given the trajectory on which the cultural narrative around the management of digital content appears to be moving, then, it is not inconceivable that the removal and delisting opportunities being gradually expanded in the present could become more the norm than the exception in the future. In such a case, the paid work of reputation management professionals would simply play less of a restorative function and assume a more traditional form of public relations image burnishing.

Index

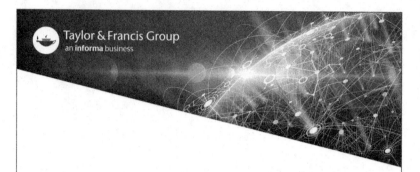

Printed in the United States
by Baker & Taylor Publisher Services